HORRIBLY ★ FAMOUS

PIRATES

...n Capers

Euston House, 24 Eversholt Street,
London NW1 1DB, UK

A division of Scholastic Ltd
London ~ New York ~ Toronto ~ Sydney ~ Auckland
Mexico City ~ New Delhi ~ Hong Kong

Published in the UK by Scholastic Ltd, 2007

Text copyright © Michael Cox 2007
Illustrations copyright © Clive Goddard, 2007

10 digit ISBN 0 439 94381 7
13 digit ISBN 978 0439 94381 9

All rights reserved
Printed in the UK by CPI Bookmarque, Croydon, CR0 4TD

2 4 6 8 10 9 7 5 3 1

CONTENTS

INTRODUCTION

Feed Long John Silver to the cat-o'-nine-tails, push Captain Pugwash into the paddling pool and tell Captain Hook to sling his curly metal mitt! Because they aren't real pirates. They're made-up characters in stories. Next to people like Horrible Henry Morgan, William Dampier, Captain Kidd, Black Bart, Anne Bonny, Mary Read and Blackbeard, they're a bunch of seagoing cuddly bunnies who would wet themselves if they ever came face-to-face with a real flesh-and-blood buccaneer.

Real pirates were a thousand times wickeder, wilder and weirder than any storybook swashbuckler. They ruled the waves, waived the rules, nobbled navies and scared seafarers shirtless from the Bahamas to Brazil and from Carolina to China.

Between 1500 and 1730, the Caribbean Sea was positively *seething* with high-seas hijackers. They swashed and buckled and rollicked and roistered like there was no tomorrow – and for many of them there wasn't, since they frequently ended up hanged, hacked, drowned or dumped on deserted islands, not to mention becoming supper for starving sharks. But, along the way, they had adventures that would make Jack Sparrow green with envy.

And, unlike pretend pirates, they didn't just prance around in namby-pamby groups of six or seven, with just one or two pathetic boats between them. Sometimes, over a thousand screaming, roaring buccaneers would sail up rivers, anchor their huge fleets of ships, then go charging into cities, blasting their blunderbusses, swinging their cutlasses and uttering curses that would make a deaf parrot blush. And what's more, some of these evil bands of crazy cut-throats were led by girls. Fearless females who ruled their gangs with wills of iron, making grown buccaneers tremble in their boots.

So if you want to find out…
- **WHY** Horrible Henry Morgan ate his own shoes
- **WHY** William Dampier walked around with a quarter of a cow hanging around his neck
- **WHY** Captain Kidd had to be hanged twice, then covered all over in tar
- **WHY** the carpet at Newgate Prison never stopped wriggling
- **WHERE** you can buy the sweetest, tastiest rats in the world
- **WHO** bit off Sadie the Goat's ear
- **HOW** a bunch of grapes finally turned Black Bart into a 'holey ghost'
- **WHY** it was incredibly important for pirates to keep their bottoms clean
- **HOW** to make pirate stink bombs
- **WHERE** Captain Kidd buried his treasure

… and boatloads more fearsome facts, stories of nautical naughtiness, not to mention murderous memoirs, just splice your main brace, weigh your anchor, set sail and prepare to meet the cut-throats of the Caribbean!

WHY BECOME A PIRATE?

1 During the times when our Horribly Famous pirates were getting up to their high-seas high-jinks, life in general was said to have been 'nasty, brutish and short' (and, most likely, so was your dad). Every day was a struggle for survival. Most people had no education, no health care, no social security and no money.

MORE COCKROACH FLAN, DEAR?

2 Disease, danger, violence and filth were everywhere. If you reached your sixth birthday, you really did have something to celebrate! Out of every 100 babies who'd managed to survive being born, 36 died before they reached the age of six.

3 If you did get to be six, not long afterwards you might find yourself working a 14-hour day on a farm or down a mine where you'd be beaten by your boss or horribly injured in one of the gruesome accidents that occurred with alarming regularity.

4 And turning to petty crime to improve your lot in life was definitely to be avoided. In those days, 'zero-tolerance' ruled, and punishments for the smallest misdeeds were horrendous. For stealing a loaf of bread, you could: **a)** be tied to a cart and whipped through the streets; **b)** be branded with a red-hot iron; **c)** have your ears nailed to the pillory while a screaming mob threw rotten food and dog poo at you; or **d)** be hung by the neck until you were extremely uncomfortable, then extremely dead. It all depended on what sort of mood the judge was in.

So, what with all that to put up with, it was no wonder 75 out of every 100 human beings died before they reached the age of 26.

Escape!

But what could you do to change your awful life of servitude and misery? What about running away to sea? Well, quite a lot of people did do that. For starters, the pay was better! If you joined the Royal Navy you might earn a whole pound every single week – twice as much as your mates slaving in the mines, muck heaps and mills. On top of that, there were those trips to exciting foreign places, not to mention all the lovely girls waiting for you in every port. And, if you still had any doubts about a life at sea, the 'press gang' would be happy to help you make up your mind.

The press gang

Press gangs usually consisted of eight or so very tough men who wandered around the ports of Britain looking for naval recruits. If you were a healthy chap, aged somewhere between 14 and 50, they would most definitely be after you as a 'volunteer' (ha!) for the Royal Navy.

In order to persuade you to 'volunteer' they would…
• Offer you the King's shilling – quite a lot of money for a pauper like you – if you took it, you'd 'volunteered'.

• Slip the King's shilling in your pocket when you weren't looking, then say…

In others words, you'd accepted payment in advance for all the work you were going to be doing in the navy.

• Buy you a pint of beer and drop the King's shilling in that – if you drank the beer, you'd volunteered! Some pubs started putting glass bottoms in their pewter tankards so people could avoid this trick. Some still have them.

• Get you so drunk that you passed out, then carry you on to the ship.

• Or, if they were feeling particularly playful, they'd simply keep the King's shilling, knock you unconscious and, next thing you knew, you'd be waking up on a warship to begin your new life of pain, misery and more pain.

The discipline in the navy was horribly strict, and once you'd been 'volunteered' there was no getting out. You did as you were told, or you suffered the consequences. Which were awful! For the smallest offence, such as being asleep on duty or stealing a bit of extra food, you could well...

• Be dangled from the rigging or spars by your arms.
• Be whipped mercilessly, then have salt and vinegar rubbed in your wounds.
• Have your finger wedged in a 25 kg weight then be made to carry it.
• Be made to swallow cockroaches.
• Have your teeth knocked out, then have an iron bolt jammed in your mouth.

These are all punishments that sailors have actually suffered in the past.

On top of all that, you'd regularly be hit by officers with canes and whips, and have to cope with storms, sickness, soakings, searing heat, freezing cold, non-stop work and the constant threat of death from disease, drowning or violence. (How does that pound a week grab you now?)

And compared to life in the *merchant* navy, the *Royal* Navy was a doddle!

So, why not escape ... again!

So there you are, onboard your ship, feeling that life can't get much worse, when it does! Suddenly, cannon are roaring and muskets cracking and dozens of pirates are swarming aboard your ship. Moments later, they have you and the rest of the crew totally at their mercy. But even the worst situations often have hidden opportunities. 'We need new recruits!' yells the pirate captain. 'Any of you jack tars fancy joining us pirates?' And then their PR (pirate recruitment) executive begins his pitch (not that there were such things in those days).

COME ON, BOYS, BE A **PIRATE** – JUST LOOK AT THE ADVANTAGES!

If you did decide to become a pirate, or 'go on account' as it was called, you could generally expect...

• Fair treatment from your superior officers and your own say in all decision-making. You and your mates could even vote for your captain to be replaced if you thought he wasn't up to the job.

GERROFF, YOU'RE RUBBISH!

SPLOOSH!

• A minimum of work – pirate ships always had *huge* crews.

• The chance to make as much as £4,000 (about £4,000,000 in today's money) in a single year – that's 12 times as much as the Governor of the mighty East India Company in Bombay was paid and a whopping great 4,000 times more than you'd get working on a farm! So, in a world where you could be hanged for stealing a shilling, you might as well go the whole 10,000 leagues and really make your crimes pay!

In addition to all these fabulous benefits, you'd also enjoy…

• A life of freedom and excitement, roaming the world's oceans, with non-stop boozing, gambling and unlimited naughtiness every time you take a 'prize' – that's pirate for captured ship.

• Lots of opportunities for revenge on all those cruel captains and other officers who've made your life in the merchant or Royal Navy a misery.

And, even if you still don't fancy the life of a sea-rover, you might well end up being a pirate when your captors make you an offer you can't refuse.

The Spanish Main

Once you'd become a pirate, if you weren't already there, you'd probably end up in the part of the world known as the Spanish Main. This was the massive Spanish-controlled empire that once included all of South and Central America and lasted for more than 300 years, providing the Spanish with more wealth than they could have amassed from winning the lottery 5,000 times a week.

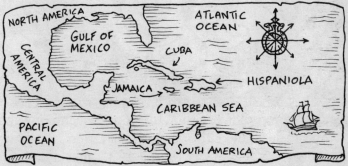

And what's more, they'd found their 'Golden Empire' more or less by accident...

After sailing across the Atlantic Ocean in 1502, not being entirely sure where he was going, Christopher Columbus bumped into the continent of South America and, quite soon afterwards, his Spanish masters went...

And they were off like a shot, torturing, slaughtering and stealing, just like the greedy, heartless, bullying conquistadors they were. By the 1600s they'd more or less conquered all of South America, enslaved the entire population, built themselves luxury towns and cities, and were sending gold and silver back to Spain by the shipload. Gold and silver that proved too tempting for the pirates known as the buccaneers. These rip-roaring, stop-at-nothing adventurers just had to get themselves a slice of all that shiny Spanish action. And what's more, countries like England – often at war with Spain – were only too keen to encourage them.

The buccaneers

The very first buccaneers were runaway servants and slaves who'd settled on the northern shores of Hispaniola and the island of Tortuga.

They were soon joined by all sorts of roughnecks, including wanted criminals, sailors who'd been thrown off their ships and political refugees.

In order to survive, these rough, tough men began hunting the wild cattle and pigs that roamed the tropical forests. They soon learned to use a 'boucan' to preserve the meat the way the local Carib indians did and, as a result, they became known as 'boucaniers' (later pronounced buccaneers).

Just in case you ever decide to run away from *your* cruel masters and live a life of adventure, freedom and non-existent personal hygiene on a tropical island, here's how to boucan…

1 Kill a cow. This is best done with a musket or bow and arrow (rather than simply punching it in the face or trying to strangle it with your bare hands).

2 Dismantle the cow into its component parts (i.e. chop it up).

3 Build the frame of green sticks that the French call a 'boucan'.

4 Make a slow-burning fire under your boucan and keep it going with animal bones and skins.

5 Lay strips of cow or pig meat on the boucan and turn them regularly until they're 'cured'. This is not 'cured' as in bringing the animal back to life, but cured as in dried out by the smoke from the fire and 'preserved'.

6 Tie the meat strips into bundles and sell them to visiting ships. You'll be able to charge six pieces of eight for every 100 strips of this highly prized grub as it's ideal for feeding sailors on long voyages. Mainly because it lasts for ages and doesn't go manky after a few days or weeks like the raw and salted

sort does. You can also sell the sailors the tallow fat from the meat so they can smear it all over their ships' hulls.

7 And finally, to help you keep up your strength, just as the buccaneers did, why not occasionally pause from your gory work to suck the delicious marrow fat from the bones of the animals you're butchering.

Putrid pirates

Personal hygiene wasn't a major issue with the buccaneers. Despite the fact that they spent months bending over stinky fires made from burning animal skin and bones, chopping up bloody meat and being attacked by huge swarms of biting flies, all in extremely hot and steamy weather, they hardly *ever* bothered to wash or change their clothes. Consequently, a typical buccaneer would look and smell something like this...

LONG FILTHY HAIR AND BEARD

PEAKED CAP TO KEEP SUN FROM EYES

EXPOSED SKIN SMEARED WITH LARD (FACTOR 100)

COWHIDE SHIRT, TROUSERS AND BOOTS – ENCRUSTED WITH DRIED COW'S BLOOD AND MARROW-BONE JELLY

INDUSTRIAL-STRENGTH BODY ODOUR

PONG

REEK

STINK

FESTER

MUSKET FOR SHOOTING COWS

HUNTING DOG

Surf wars

The Spanish colonizers of the West Indies hated the buccaneers and tried to get rid of them by attacking them and killing the cattle they depended on for a living. So the buccaneers fought back. Whenever a Spanish ship passed their strongholds they would leap into the dugout canoes they called pirogues and paddle like crazy through the surf until they caught up with it. Being sure-shot marksmen they found it quite easy to stand up in their rocking boats and pick off the ship's helmsman and anyone else daft enough to stick their head up. Then, once they reached the ship, they'd jam its rudder, clamber aboard, kill the Spanish and steal whatever they could. Not long after this they extended their operations by converting captured Spanish vessels into fully fledged pirate ships and began roving further and further across the seas to look for victims. They quickly gained a fearsome reputation throughout the Caribbean, becoming known as the Brethren of the Coast. And eventually, under the command of cunning rogues like our first Horribly Famous Pirate, Sir Henry Morgan, entire armies of these bloodthirsty buccaneers began attacking the vast and mind-bogglingly wealthy Spanish Main itself!

HORRIBLE HENRY MORGAN AND HIS DASHED CUNNING TRICKS 1635–1688

After having a high old time on their vicious voyages, most pirates met a miserable end by being hunted down and blown to bits or dangled from the gallows. But not the first of our Horribly Famous ocean-going gangsters, Horrible Henry Morgan. As well as successfully stealing vast amounts of treasure *and* getting to keep it, he was even given a *knighthood* for doing it! And that's not all! As *Sir* Henry Morgan, great British seafarer and national hero, he was put in charge of one of England's richest and most important colonies. *And* he had a brand of rum named after him! How did he do it? Well, Henry pulled off his many astonishing feats by being very courageous. And very, very cunning. (Not to mention horrendously ... cruel!)

Mind my pike!

Henry was born in Wales in 1635, or thereabouts. His uncles were army bigwigs so, when he left school, he decided to become a soldier. Later in his life (possibly as

21

an excuse for making a hash of his SATs) he said something like…

> I LEFT SCHOOL TOO EARLY TO BE GOOD AT LEARNING AND HAVE BECOME BETTER AT USING THE PIKE THAN THE BOOK.

NB: It's assumed he was talking about the weapon, and not the fish – however one never knows.

> GET BACK OR MY ENORMOUS FEROCIOUS FRESHWATER FISH WILL BITE YOU TO PIECES!

> AH! RUN AWAY!

In 1654, along with about 7,000 other British adventurers, Henry took part in the invasion of the Spanish colony of Hispaniola*, but the expedition failed because lots of them were killed by the Spanish or caught nasty tropical diseases (and they were rubbish anyway). However, a bit later on, they did manage to capture Jamaica from the Spanish and turn it into an English colony. Henry was soon leading expeditions from Jamaica against the Spaniards on the South American mainland. He got himself a reputation as a cunning leader and

* Second largest island in the Caribbean and part of Spain's massive Golden Empire. Now divided up into Haiti and the Dominican Republic.

courageous fighter. Then, at the age of 32, after gaining the respect of buccaneers everywhere, he became Admiral of that bloodthirsty bunch of Spaniard-slayers known as the Brethren of the Coast.

Horrible Henry's hyper-heist

In 1668, Horrible Henry and his buccaneer buddies decided to do something that everyone else thought was impossible! They made up their minds to conquer the Spanish city of Porto Bello on the coast of Costa Rica. Porto Bello was packed with warehouses full to bursting with gold and silver, all waiting to be picked up by Spanish galleons and transported back to old Spain. And Henry wanted that gold and silver. However, when older, more experienced pirates heard of his plan to attack this formidable fortress city, they said that it would be suicide to try. But they'd reckoned without Henry's stunning cunning and utter ruthlessness. He was determined to get what he wanted.

MORGAN'S MURDEROUS MEMOIRS

10 July 1668: I'm going to take Porto Bello. But it won't be easy. Huge forts manned by hundreds of soldiers guard the entrance to the bay. Anyone trying to approach from the ocean would be blown to smithereens by their cannon. But I've got a dashed cunning trick...

Morgan's dashed cunning tricks

I sailed my fleet to a spot some miles down the coast, transferred 500 of my pirates into 23 canoes. Then, under cover of darkness, we paddled our way up the coast, landed a few miles from the city, sneaked through the jungle and surprised them from behind! They weren't expecting us, because they didn't believe anyone was brave enough to attack them. Well, they had a surprise coming!

11 July 1688: It worked! Two of the forts and Porto Bello were taken. The local folk were petrified when we charged down their main street yelling like banshees and firing our muskets and flintlocks.

Those muskets and flintlocks were terrifying, as were all pirate weapons. And the buccaneers had dozens to choose from. Find out about them in…

WICKED WEAPONS

Flash! Bang! Wallop!: Hand guns

• Musket: Long gun, usually fired from the shoulder, which could hit a human target from about 100 metres away. Once it had been fired it had to be reloaded. This fiddly operation involved pirates holding the bullets in their teeth then 'spitting' them into the musket barrel. This was, of course, a disadvantage.

WHAT DO YOU MEAN, YOU'VE JUST SWALLOWED YOUR LAST BULLET?

• Blunderbuss (nothing to do with useless public transport): A one-man cannon also known as the 'thunder gun'. When fired they recoiled (i.e. 'kicked back') with the power of a kangaroo. Used for boarding parties and for personal defence.

WATCH THIS THEN!

BOOM!

• Flintlock pistol: Buccaneers fired their fearsome flintlocks whenever they were boarding and in close-up fights. They could be tricky in hand-to-hand scraps because, like the musket, once they'd fired just one shot, the buccaneers would have to reload immediately.

> DO YOU MIND HANGING ON A MINUTE WHILE I RELOAD?

> NO PROBS, MATE.

If there wasn't time to reload, pirates used their gun's butt-end to 'pistol-whip' their foes.
• Powder-box, horn or flask made of wood, leather, or ivory: Pirates used these to keep their powder in and ensure it stayed dry. If they used damp powder they simply got a flash-in-the-pan, i.e. a disappointing result. Wearing a powder box in a scrap could be dangerous…

STRAY SPARK + POWDER HORN + BUCCANEER = PULVERISED PIRATE

BOOOOM!

MORGAN'S MURDEROUS MEMOIRS

11 July 1688 (continued): We're in Porto Bello all right, but these pesky Spaniards have hidden their gold and silver! Though I'm sure they'll be happy to tell us where it all is when we've tortured them a bit. The richer ones and the governor have now taken refuge behind the high, well-defended walls of the inner fort. Which is going to be a much harder nut to crack! The Spanish are determined we aren't going to get in. But I can already feel a cruel and audacious plan coming on! They don't call me 'Morgan The Terrible' for nothing! Ha ha ha (<evil laughter>) ha ha ha!

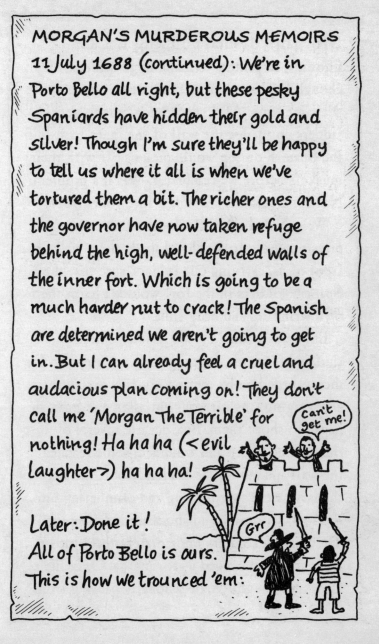

Later: Done it!
All of Porto Bello is ours.
This is how we trounced 'em:

Morgan's dashed cunning tricks

I got my carpenters to make huge ladders, wide enough for four men to stand on one rung at the same time. All I needed now was to get the ladders up against the wall of the inner fort. But the Spanish on top would pick us off with their muskets before we reached it. Was it a problem? Not for a ruthless scoundrel like yours truly!

We rounded up all the local monks, nuns, priests and old folk. Then I made them walk in front of us, carrying our ladders, sure that the Spanish soldiers in the fort wouldn't harm their own wrinklies and holy folk.

But I was wrong! As my 'human shield' shuffled forwards, begging their countrymen for mercy, urged on by me and my lads giving them encouraging jabs with our cutlasses, the Spanish began to shoot them. But, despite several of them being killed and wounded, some reached the wall and put up the ladders. Soon, me and the boys were swarming up and clambering into the fort, screaming and shooting and stabbing! The Spanish soldiers immediately threw down their arms and begged us for mercy. Only their Governor fought on, occasionally pausing from battling us to kill a few of his own men for being such wimps!

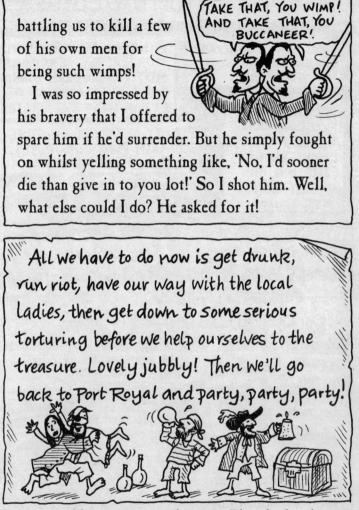

TAKE THAT, YOU WIMP! AND TAKE THAT, YOU BUCCANEER'.

I was so impressed by his bravery that I offered to spare him if he'd surrender. But he simply fought on whilst yelling something like, 'No, I'd sooner die than give in to you lot!' So I shot him. Well, what else could I do? He asked for it!

All we have to do now is get drunk, run riot, have our way with the local ladies, then get down to some serious torturing before we help ourselves to the treasure. Lovely jubbly! Then we'll go back to Port Royal and party, party, party!

Pirates couldn't stay at sea for ever. They had to have a place where they could spend their ill-gotten gains and have fun, without worrying that they might be arrested and strung up. There were several of these 'safe havens' dotted around the world. Welcome to…

PIRATE PARADISES: PORT ROYAL, JAMAICA

PORT ROYAL HARBOUR-BIG ENOUGH TO HOLD 500 SHIPS

A HANG-OUT FOR ASSORTED MURDERERS, MERCHANTS, MISFITS, MUGGERS, MANIACS AND A HUGE AMOUNT OF EX-CONVICTS - AND PIRATES!

ENTERTAINMENTS INCLUDING BULL AND BEAR BAITING, COCK-FIGHTING, GAMBLING AND BINGO. (POSSIBLY NOT BINGO)

PLENTY OF STREET-FIGHTING, DRUNKEN PUNCH-UPS, DUELS, STABBINGS AND ALL-IN-WRESTLING

GETTING POSITIVELY PLASTERED

HIC!

YO-HO-HO AND A ROTTLE OF BUM!

THEY'RE MOUTH-WATERINGLY SWEET AND JUICY!

EXTRA TASTY SUGAR CANE RATS

SPECIAL TODAY-PIRATE RAT PIE WITH REAL PIE-RATS

YUM, YUM!

DOCKSIDE STALLS SELLING EXOTIC GOODS

Not to be missed! The return of a pirate ship:

The big cannon at Fort Charles is fired to signal the victorious return of a boatload of buccaneers. Everyone drops what they're doing and dashes to the docks.

The pirate ship is tied up, the King's officials go on board for their ten per cent of the booty. Businessmen who've 'sponsored' the expedition get their slice of the action.

The buccaneers give out free rum. Everyone drinks. The buccaneers auction their plunder to the sozzled public.

It only took Henry's betting, battling, brothel-going, binge-drinking buccaneers a few months to blow their booty in Port Royal. By October they were broke and desperate to go plundering again…

Realizing that this was another opportunity for him to increase his vast wealth, not to mention impressing the bigwigs back home in England, Horrible Henry spread the word that there was going to be a huge buccaneer meeting at Cow Island off the coast of Hispaniola. So, in January 1669, 800 buccaneers on 12 ships got together and began to plot all manner of mischief. Then, after they'd made their plans, Henry and his buccaneer pals decided to 'pre-celebrate' the great victories they were convinced would soon be theirs. It wasn't a good idea…

Horrible Henry's big bang-quet

All the buccaneers began boozing and drinking toasts. Then they had a few more drinks while Henry and his captains retired to his admiral's cabin for a slap-up banquet.

Meanwhile, the other buccaneers carried on boozing and several of the more excitable ones began firing their muskets in the air. Some sparks landed on the ship's gunpowder supply and next moment there was an almighty…

The ship and the buccaneers were blown sky high. More than 300 of them were blasted to pieces. However, Henry had an amazing stroke of luck. Along with all the captains who'd been sitting on his side of the table, he escaped with hardly a scratch. But the ones on the other side of it were blown to bits!

A few days after the disaster, Henry and his chums began fishing bodies of out of the sea. Not because they wanted to give their pals a decent burial. They just wanted their clothes and jewellery! Once they'd stripped their pals and chopped off their hands for their rings, they threw them back in the sea for the sharks to enjoy.

Murder and mayhem in Maracaibo

Horrible Henry definitely wasn't going to be put off by a little mishap like an exploding ship and the death of 300 buccaneers. After assembling a fleet of eight ships and gathering a pirate army of almost 1,000 cut-throats, he made his way to the lakeside city of Maracaibo on the coast of Venezuela.

But when they got there, they discovered the Spaniards had run away, sensibly taking their gold and silver with them, or burying it in the jungle so that they could come back for it later.

Henry was very, very angry! For the next three weeks he sent out marauding parties who would return at the end of each day leading mules loaded with loot, followed by long lines of the miserable Spanish men, women and children who they'd taken prisoner. Then, under Horrible Henry's instructions, the bloodthirsty buccaneers set about torturing their pathetic captives to make them reveal where they'd stashed their silver and savings. Here are some of the dastardly things they did to them...

• Strappado: The buccaneers tied their victims' arms behind their backs, threw the rope over a high beam, then pulled it so violently that the poor wretches were yanked into the air. If Horrible Henry and his murderous mates were feeling playful, they would jerk the person up and down a bit, or even tie big rocks to their feet.

• Woolding: This charming trick involved Henry and his buccaneers wrapping a thin rope around their victim's head, then twisting it around a stick until his or her eyes… No, no it's just too horrible to go on!

• Stretching: This was done on the torture machines known as racks. There were plenty of these around because the equally cruel Spaniards regularly used them on local native American Indians, just to remind them who was in charge.

After creating mayhem and misery around Maracaibo, Henry and his monstrous mob moved to the Venezuelan town of Gibraltar. And began all over again! For instance, in order to get one old chap to tell them where his money was, Henry's henchmen spreadeagled him between four stakes, placed a boulder on chest and lit a fire underneath him.

Makes you really proud to be British, doesn't it?

After spending several weeks waging woe on the Spanish, Horrible Henry decided to return to Port Royal with his plunder. However, he was in for a surprise. While he and his buccaneers had been looting, torturing and murdering, the Spanish authorities had been busy. They were determined he wasn't going to get away with his booty.

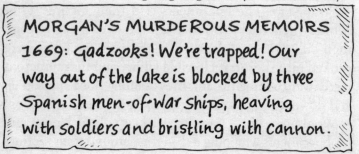

MORGAN'S MURDEROUS MEMOIRS
1669: Gadzooks! We're trapped! Our way out of the lake is blocked by three Spanish men-of-war ships, heaving with soldiers and bristling with cannon.

In a straight fight we won't stand a chance. They'll blow us out of the water.

But I didn't get where I am today by straight fighting. This situation most definitely calls for one of my famous rascally ruses.

Morgan's dashed cunning tricks

I decided that what we needed was a 'fire ship', a blazing boat to sail straight into the Spanish ships and cause chaos. But not just any old fire ship. In order to fool the Spaniards, we disguised it as an admiral's flagship! Here's how...

· We placed big logs with pumpkins on top around the deck of a captured ship. We dressed them in buccaneers' hats and clothes and gave them cutlasses and muskets so that they looked like pirates.

· We collected hundreds of palm-tree leaves and covered them with tar and brimstone, then piled them up in the hold of our fire ship along with lots of other things that would burn really well.

· My buccaneers made new portholes in the sides of the fire ship, then poked big hollow logs out of the holes so that they looked like cannon.

· They then slathered the 'cannon' in more tar and brimstone and put six pots of gunpowder under each one.

· We flew an admiral-of-the-fleet's flag from the fire ship's main mast.

· We floated a ship carrying burning ropes at the rear of our ships so that the Spaniards would think this was the real fire ship, rather than the pretend flagship, which was really the fire ship.

NOW, THIS IS THE <u>REAL</u> FLAGSHIP, AND THIS IS THE FIRE SHIP WHICH IS <u>PRETENDING</u> TO BE THE FLAGSHIP AND THIS IS THE <u>PRETEND</u> FIRE SHIP.

NO, WE STILL DON'T GET IT...

· And finally, 12 of my bravest (or stupidest) buccaneers volunteered to stay aboard the fire ship, steer it towards the Spaniards, catch hold of their man o' war with grappling irons, then light burning fuses and leap into the sea at the very last moment.

Henry's trick worked. It was only when the fire ship was right alongside the biggest Spanish man-of-war that the Spanish commander realized he'd been tricked. He immediately ordered his men to cut down the fire ship's masts and push it away. But too late! There was a massive explosion and next moment burning sails and timbers were pouring down on the Spanish ship. Moments later it caught fire too! As its crew leapt into the sea, the second Spanish man-of-war fled towards the safety of the fort but became stuck in shallow water. Its crew immediately set it on fire and abandoned ship, too. In the meantime, the third ship was boarded and captured by Henry and his buccaneers. But they still couldn't escape from the lake. Try as they might, they couldn't defeat the Spaniards in the fort who bombarded them with all sorts of explosive nasties.

MORGAN'S MURDEROUS MEMOIRS

So there we were! Still trapped in that lake with all our lovely money and treasure. I was going to have to think of yet another brilliant ruse to fool the Spaniards. But I didn't get where I am today by not being one courageous, scheming son-of-a-gun! So here's what I did next.

Morgan's dashed cunning tricks

I got my oarsmen to ferry canoe-loads of pirates from our ships to the wooded shore below the fort. Back and forth they went, all day long, carrying one canoe-load after another. By evening it seemed as if my entire buccaneer army had been ferried to the shore and hidden in the jungle. But had they? Had they thuggery! They hadn't even got out of the cotton-picking canoes. As soon as they were hidden in the cover of the trees, they'd simply stretched themselves out in the bottom of the boats and been ferried back to our ships.

It certainly fooled the Spaniards. All day long they'd been counting the men who were being 'landed' in the jungle. By evening they were convinced that there must have been hundreds of us hidden there, all ready to launch a huge night attack on them from the land. So what did they do? They trundled all their massive cannon from one side of the fort to the other so that they faced the jungle, in preparation for our 'night attack'! In other words, pointing away from our ships! Which is exactly what I'd hoped they'd do!

As soon as it got dark, we raised our anchors and floated towards the fort on the high tide. Then, the moment we were level with it, we hoisted our sails and made our way to the open sea. Once they realized they'd been tricked, the Spanish rushed to shift their guns back to the side of the fort facing the lake. But by this time we were well away. So I fired them a seven cannon 'cheerio' salute. Sarcastic ... or what? And then it was back to Port Royal for more merrymaking.

Way to go Morgan, me bucko!

Horrible Henry's final fling!

In 1670 Henry decided to have a bash at capturing the biggest prize of all: the fabulously rich Spanish city of Panama. Panama was Spain's pride and joy, the wealthiest city in all its vast South American empire. It was packed with palaces and mansions, luxury villas belonging to rich Spanish merchants, a treasury overflowing with gold and silver, as well as a great cathedral full of fantastically valuable religious ornaments. All Henry needed now was an excuse to attack it. And it didn't take him long to think of one. Of course! It was a threat to his home territory of Jamaica. For all he knew, at this very moment, the Spanish in Panama might be planning to invade Port Royal! Henry decided to get his retaliation in first.

News of his plans soon spread around the Caribbean and, in no time at all, more than 2,000 of the most dangerous and bloodthirsty buccaneers in the West Indies flocked to him, eager to join his expedition. He soon assembled a fleet of 36 ships to transport these cut-throats to the Isthmus of Darien, the narrow strip of land that separated the Caribbean Sea from the Pacific Ocean.

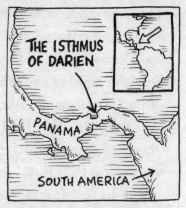

Henry's plan was to travel through the jungle by river, then attack Panama from the land. And this meant sending a group of buccaneers to attack the fort that guarded the entrance to the river. It was well defended and after more than 150 of his buccaneers had been killed or wounded in the battle to take it, it looked like they were going to fail. But they had a stroke of luck.

Partway through the battle, a buccaneer was hit by an arrow. Feeling rather cut up about it, he immediately seized the arrow, ripped it out of his body, wrapped it in cotton cloth, stuffed it into his musket barrel and shot it back at the fort. By the time it landed on the palm-leaf roof of one of the houses, the arrow was ablaze, having been ignited by the gunpowder in the musket. The fire soon spread to other houses and then to a gunpowder store, which exploded, causing the Spaniards to turn their attention from defending the fort. This was the chance the buccaneers had been waiting for. They charged the fort and set fire to the wooden stockade. Not long afterwards, victory was theirs.

Henry and 1,200 of his pirates now clambered into a fleet of canoes and other small boats and began to paddle their way up the river towards the fabulous city of Panama. However, their progress was painfully slow. Because of the hundreds of tortuous twists and turns in the river, they would often paddle for hours, then pass the exact spot they had been at earlier in the day.

Soon, the river became too shallow to navigate, so Henry abandoned the canoes and the buccaneers began to hack their way through the dense tropical jungle.

Henry's green hell

With modern survival kits, hi-tech clothing, global positioning systems, maps, and specialist food and medicine, dense tropical jungles can still be horrendously difficult to travel through, even for experienced and determined explorers. To move just a few hundred metres can sometimes take an entire day, while the stifling heat and humidity quickly leaves the fittest trekkers exhausted and gasping for breath. So for Henry and his buccaneers, who had no modern equipment, supplies, maps or medicine, the whole thing rapidly turned into a nightmare.

• Vicious thorns and spikes ripped their thin leather shoes from their feet and their clothes from their bodies, then began tearing at their exposed flesh.

• They were attacked by biting insects and creepy-crawlies, including bloodsucking leeches, poisonous spiders and swarms of bees.

• Poisonous snakes and hungry alligators attacked without warning. As stricken pirates screamed in terror they were simply abandoned by their mates.

• Hostile native Indians would regularly ambush the buccaneers, shooting them with poison-tipped arrows.

• Every day the buccaneers were drenched by torrential rain then scorched by the blazing sun.

• Being constantly sweaty, they suffered from the horrid itchy condition known as crotch rot, caused by fungus growing in all their most sensitive spots.

• Then, as if all this wasn't bad enough, they began to suffer from lots and lots of disgusting ... diseases!

The poorly pirate

In the days before tablets and vaccinations, pirates caught all sorts of diseases and fell ill by the boatload. Most pirate ships returned from voyages with only half their crew, the rest having died from illness. This is why most pirates were in their 20s. By the time they reached their 30s they were either dead or worn out. Here's just one of the many nasties that Henry and his men suffered from:

DISGUSTING DISEASES — THE BLOODY FLUX

The modern name for this disease is dysentery (but that doesn't make it any less disgusting). For hundreds of extremely unsanitary centuries the bloody flux has killed millions and millions of people all over the world, including thousands of seafarers and pirates, a famous one being Elizabethan swashbuckler Sir Francis Drake.

CAUSES: Not washing your hands after you've been to the loo. Drinking contaminated water. Eating food that has been prepared by someone who doesn't wash their hands when they've been to the loo.

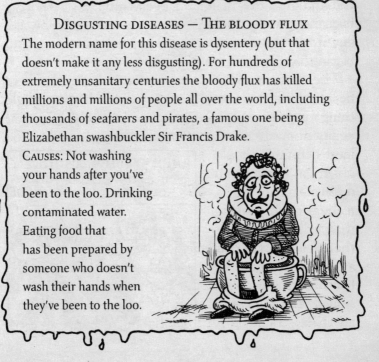

SYMPTOMS: Constant bloody diarrhoea. Agonizing stomach pains. Death.

CURE: There isn't one. However, pirates and similarly ignorant nitwits believed that they could get better by all sorts of bizarre remedies, including:
a) sitting on something hot;
b) eating nutmeg or opium;
or c) pushing the pointy end of a hot, hard-boiled egg up their bottom.

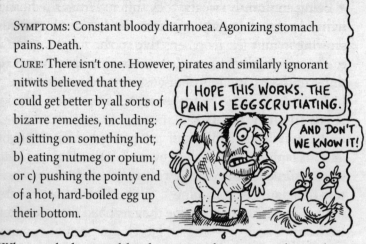

What with diseases like dysentery, the insects, the snakes, the Indians, the heat and everything else, Henry's buccaneers were thinking matters couldn't possibly get any worse. But then they did. They ran out of food and began to starve to death.

The Spanish villagers and native Indians who were fleeing them made sure that they didn't leave a single thing for them to eat. Desperate to put anything in their empty stomachs, the buccaneers did something that you most definitely should not try at home, even if you are feeling really, really peckish! Having thoroughly 'tenderized' their leather satchels and leftover shoes by beating them with stones, they boiled and ate them!

After enduring ten days of this green hell, during which more than 200 of them died, Henry and his scarecrow army finally emerged from the jungle and saw the towers and rooftops of Panama shimmering in the distance. Not long afterwards, the ravenous rovers had a lucky find. Well, lucky for them, but not quite so lucky for the herd of donkeys and cows that they slaughtered and roasted. And, being so desperately hungry, they didn't even wait for the meat to cook. They simply stuffed huge chunks of raw donkey flesh and steak into their mouths, tearing and gnawing at it like wild animals, as the blood drenched their beards and clothes. Then, looking like a horde of jungle vampires, with their beards and rags soaked in blood, they began to advance on Panama.

Morgan's dashed cunning tricks

Lined up between us and our prize were more than 3,000 Spanish soldiers. Yes, we were outnumbered by three to one! Instead of simply charging the Spaniards head-on and being cut to pieces by their cavalry, I split my buccaneers into four squadrons. Then I ordered one of the squadrons to wheel to the left and capture the hill that overlooked the city. When this squadron moved away from the main body of my men, the Spanish immediately thought we were retreating. The whole lot of them, cavalry and foot soldiers both, charged us. Well, for my crackshot buccaneers, it was like shooting fish in a barrel. Pow! Pow! Bang! Bang! Down they went by the dozen.

But then, above the sound of musket fire, I suddenly heard a deafening roar! I turned to see Spanish slaves stampeding a huge herd of bulls towards us from the rear. There must have been at least 2,000 of the massive beasts. Normal folk would have fled in terror. But not me and my bold buccaneers. Stampeding bulls weren't going to faze the best cattle-killers in the Caribbean. As cool as cucumbers, we calmly turned and fired, instantly bringing dozens of the bulls crashing to the ground. Just seconds later, the rest of the maddened beasts turned and thundered back towards the slaves and their Spanish masters, trampling them into a bloody mush! The day was ours!

Take the money ... and run!

Not wanting their city to fall into the buccaneers' bloody hands, the Spanish citizens set it on fire and ran away to hide in the woods. Three-quarters of Panama was destroyed, including a fort containing 40 soldiers who didn't get out quickly enough. Henry got treasure, but not as much as he'd expected. He also missed a few choice pieces – for instance, an enormous golden cross that a Spanish priest had covered in white paint so he didn't notice it.

Anyway, the main thing was that, after going through all those terrible experiences, Henry's buccaneer army weren't going to get as much loot as they'd expected. Soon there were mutinous mutterings amongst the ranks and Henry realized that if he wanted to escape with his life he'd have to pull a fast one.

Morgan's dashed cunning tricks

I told all the buccaneers that, after doing the sums, there was only enough for each of them to get 200 pieces of eight each. They were not well pleased! I was sure they would mutiny. So here's what I did. In the dead of night, My closest chums and I slipped our ship's anchor and headed for the open seas, along with most of the loot. I'm a cunning old dog, aren't I? When we got back to Port Royal, we divided up the money. Naturally, the biggest shares went to myself (£100,000) and the King (£1,000,000).

Dunplunderin'!

With Henry providing him with 'tasty little earners' like that, it's hardly surprising that King Charles II made him *Sir Henry* and Governor of Jamaica. Which meant he could give up pirating and retire to his 6,000-acre Jamaican country estate. As his slaves toiled away cutting sugar cane, he lay in a hammock – eating and boozing and swelling to the size of a small hot-air balloon. After becoming really poorly from his pigging out, he was treated by a local doctor who tried all sorts of cures, including making him drink oil made from crushed scorpions, plastering him all over with clay and water, and washing his insides out with someone else's wee. Not surprisingly, he died soon afterwards. On 25 August 1688, two Royal Navy warships anchored in Port Royal fired cannon salutes to him and he was buried in Port Royal churchyard. But he wasn't going to stay there long!

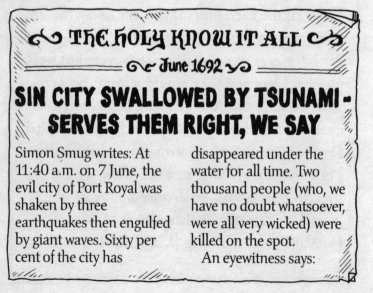

◇◇ THE HOLY KNOW IT ALL ◇◇
◇◇ June 1692 ◇◇

SIN CITY SWALLOWED BY TSUNAMI – SERVES THEM RIGHT, WE SAY

Simon Smug writes: At 11:40 a.m. on 7 June, the evil city of Port Royal was shaken by three earthquakes then engulfed by giant waves. Sixty per cent of the city has disappeared under the water for all time. Two thousand people (who, we have no doubt whatsoever, were all very wicked) were killed on the spot.

An eyewitness says:

There was this horrible rumbling and the earth opened up, instantly swallowing people and leaving only their heads poking above the ground. Seconds later the ground closed up again, squeezing the screaming wretches to death but still leaving their heads visible.

AT LEAST THINGS CAN'T GET ANY WORSE...

But worse was to come! Some time later starving dogs hunting for food found the heads and ate them!

Coffins and bodies burst from graves in the churchyard and were soon floating in the harbour. We have now learned that at least 2,000 more people have died from disease and injuries since the disaster. All we can say is: serves them all right for being so badly behaved. It doesn't pay to go annoying 'Him up there'...

QUITE SO!

ISN'T THAT OLD HENRY MORGAN?

IF IT IS, HE'S LOST AN AWFUL LOT OF WEIGHT!

51

WILLIAM DAMPIER AND HIS AWFULLY BIG ADVENTURES
The brainy buccaneer 1651–1715

Most pirates did roving, roughing-up, robbing, roistering and rum-drinking. And that was about it. But a few, like William Dampier, did a bit more than that. Or, in William's case, a LOT more!

In addition to being a buccaneer, William was an explorer, a best-selling author, a scientist, a map maker, a botanist, a hydrographer* and a naturist…

Sorry, a *naturalist*! Oh yes, and talking of using the right words, he also found time to introduce over 1,000 new ones to the English language.

* Someone who makes maps of the oceans to make navigation easier.

Whizz-kid William was born near Yeovil in Somerset in 1651. His dad was a prosperous farmer who made sure William got a good education, which included subjects like English, drawing, Latin and maths. However, when he was only seven, his dad died. Seven years later, his mum died of the plague and William went to live with guardians.

William was a clever lad who was interested in everything around him and desperate to see more of the world. So when he became a teenager, he asked his carers if he could become a shipmaster's apprentice in Weymouth. They agreed and William went a-roving…

First I sailed to France and back – 100 miles. Then I sailed across the Atlantic Ocean to Newfoundland and back – 5,000 miles. But I decided I didn't like sailing in northern waters as it was freezing cold.

So I made sure the next ship I sailed on was going somewhere warm and I sailed to Java and back – a mere 17,000 miles Then I joined the Royal Navy and took part in two huge sea battles with the Dutch but, during a third battle, I fell ill and went home to Somerset. Then, at the ripe old age of 22, I decided that I was ready for my first really BIG adventure.

William's first really big adventure

After he'd recovered from his illness, one of William's Somerset neighbours asked him if he fancied helping to manage his sugar plantation in Jamaica, so he said… and off he went to the West Indies. Unfortunately, he didn't get on with the plantation boss and they ended up fighting. Consequently, in 1675, William suddenly found himself 4,000 miles from home, out of work, out of money and with nowhere to live, so he said something like…

NOT HALF!

WHATEVER! I'LL GO AND BE A LOGWOODER!

And, not long after that, he bumped into the buccaneers!

See you later, alligator!

The place William went to join the logwooders was the Bay of Campeachy, in the country that is now known as Belize. Logwood grew in the mangrove swamps there and could be sold for huge amounts of money back in Europe where it was highly prized for the brilliant red dye it produced. But cutting it was incredibly dangerous and hard work. Almost all of the logwooders were ex-buccaneers who'd been in the pirate army of Horrible Henry Morgan.

But because Henry and the conniving English bigwigs who'd encouraged them to murder, maim and pillage now found it more convenient to be 'anti-pirate' the buccaneers suddenly found themselves out of work. So they turned to logwooding and cow-killing, while still doing the odd bit of buccaneering on the side.

Dampier's Daily Diary:
Summer 1675

We work all day long, thigh-deep in the stinking swamp water. The sun beats down on us, leeches suck the blood from our flesh and swarms of mosquitoes drive us batty with their buzzing and biting. And all the time we have to watch for the ferocious alligators which strike without warning, ripping off a man's leg with one snap of their gigantic jaws.

My back aches, my arms and hands are stained bright red and my hair and skin reek of the stinky logwood flowers. As well as the alligators, we have to watch out for the Spanish. They think this logwood belongs to them. Every now and again they carry off some poor wretched logwooder and torture him horribly before making him their slave.

I would have thought they'd be really

relieved that all my pals here have given up pirating, and just let us be.

At the end of the day we fall into our beds exhausted. But then we have to be very careful not to fall out of our beds! Because they stand on stilts in the swamp water!

WHAT DO YOU MEAN, YOU THINK YOU 'MAY HAVE WET THE BED?

They say that travel broadens your mind. It blows my mind! Here are just a few of the amazing things I have done and discovered in the past few weeks.
1) Wild-cow hunting with the logwooders: Four of us go off to hunt cows. When we have shot one we take out its bones and cut it into quarters. Then (and this is the really weird bit!) we make a hole in the meat and put our head through it to carry it back to camp. I feel like I am wearing a big beefy frock!

DOES MY RUMP LOOK BIG IN THIS?

2) A creature the size of a little pig they call an armadillo, because it is covered in armour! When cooked properly they are absolutely delicious!

3) Horned spiders as big as your fist. Us logwooders use the spiders' horns to pick meat from between our teeth and clean our tobacco pipes.

4) Ferocious black spider-monkeys that look like little old men. I came across 30 of them the other day and they began screaming and hurling their poo and squirting their wee at me. I ran away!

What an amazing world we live in. I hope to see more of it!

William did see more of the world. In fact, he became the first British person to sail around it three times. He was also the first person to make maps showing the direction of the main winds and currents of the world's oceans. He made notes about everything he saw and brought back lots of plant and animal specimens and drawings for scientists to marvel over back in England. In addition to all that, he wrote the first-ever best-selling travel books. He became the first Englishman to set foot in Australia, 80 years before Captain Cook. (In fact, when Cook went exploring he took all of William's books with him and used them as guides.) He sampled the food of all the amazing and exotic places he visited and was the first Englishman to describe tasting things like soy sauce and Thai food. His accounts of his voyages and adventures inspired famous novelists like Jonathan Swift and Daniel Defoe. He introduced hundreds of new words to the English language, including avocado, barbecue and chopsticks. He even inspired Charles Darwin to study the Galapagos Islands and come up with his theory of evolution.

WE'LL NEED CHOPSTICKS AT THE BARBECUE, AND WE'RE HAVING AVOCADO.

And of course, in between all this, he did lots and lots of pirating. Phew!

Dampier's Daily Diary
June 1676 – Disaster! Three days ago, I noticed huge numbers of men o'war birds flocking over the logwood forest – a most unusual sight! Five minutes later all the water drained out of the swamp! Then, at four o'clock in the afternoon, the sky went

black, the wind howled and a hyper-hurricane came howling in, flattening our huts, tearing all the trees from the ground and bringing a great tide of water rushing through the forest. We clambered into our one remaining canoe and only just escaped with our lives. We are now sheltering on Beef Island. I have just been chased by an alligator. This life is a hard one. But I am never bored!

A few weeks later:
The hurricane has finished my logwooding adventure for good. I am broke and homeless yet again. So my pals and I have joined the buccaneers.

Spring 1678 - Today 60 of us buccaneers attacked a Spanish fort near Vera Cruz. After a fierce and bloody battle in which 12 of my comrades were killed, we were finally victorious. But when we got inside the fort we discovered that all the rich merchants had escaped up the river with their gold and silver. All they'd left behind were hundreds of lovely red and yellow parrots. They talk beautifully (but only in Spanish)! We have so many cages of parrots on our boat that we can hardly move or hear ourselves speak above their squawking!

¡OLA!

1678 Back in England for a break from adventuring. Have also got married. My new wife is called Judith.

Back in a couple of jiffies, dear!

In 1679, after being married just a short while, William told his new wife he was off on swift business trip to Jamaica and would be back in a few months. But his return was somewhat delayed...

OH DEAR, I WONDER WHAT CAN BE KEEPING WILLIAM? HIS TEA'S GETTING COLD.

1683

HMM, STILL NOT BACK...

1688

DARLING, I'M HOME!

WHAT TOOK YOU SO LONG?

WELL, YOU'RE NOT GOING TO BELIEVE THIS. BUT...

1691

During his *twelve and a half years* away, William had hundreds of amazing adventures, including taking part in dozens of buccaneering raids and battles, getting shipwrecked, being marooned on a tropical island, and visiting loads of strange and exotic lands including China, Australia, Peru, Sumatra and the Spice Islands. All the time he was away he kept a journal, drawing and writing about all the things he saw and experienced each day. And, despite all the storms, shipwrecks and sea battles, he managed to keep his precious notes dry by putting them in bamboo tubes sealed with wax.

Dampier's Daily Diary

1679: Somewhere in the jungle: Another adventure! 330 of us buccaneers are crossing the Isthmus of Darien to Panama City, just like Sir Henry Morgan did in 1671. We are after Spanish gold! 250 local Kuna Indians armed with bows and arrows are guiding us through the jungle because they hate the Spanish. Today we arrived at the Kuna village and met their king. He has a gold plate in his nose and huge gold earrings. His daughter has been kidnapped by the Spanish and he wants revenge.

A few weeks later. Exhausted. We crossed the same twisting river 50 times today!

Early 1680. Santa Maria: We have attacked the Spanish town and rescued the king's daughter. The Kuna are torturing and killing the Spanish in revenge for her bad treatment. Uuurgh!

April 1680: Bay of Panama: We were attacked by 5 Spanish ships today. There was a three-hour sea battle with much screaming, horrible wounding and dying. Eventually we used an old buccaneer trick of rowing our canoes to one of the Spanish boats and jamming the rudder. Then we boarded it and killed nearly all of them. On one of the other ships, our comrades exploded gunpowder barrels. This led to more screaming and men running about on fire. 18 of our men were killed and 22 were wounded. Captain Harris, our leader was shot in his legs. Our ship's surgeon sawed one of them off, but the gangrene set in and he died. The smell was terrible!

Disgusting diseases — gangrene

Causes: Pirates frequently got wounds and burns when they were working and fighting. They also spent most of their time in the Tropics, where the air is positively humming with lively bacteria that like nothing better than to pig out on a bit of bashed-up or scorched flesh. And if you think our heroic antibodies will zap the germs, forget it! Blood carrying them can't get to the site of the wound because the veins all around it are too damaged for it to flow through.

Symptoms: Once the bacteria get busy, your flesh begins to decay and, as the rot sets in, it spreads at a scary three centimetres an hour! It also smells extremely unpleasant.

Cure: Cut away the infected area as quickly as possible. This often involved the amputation of limbs. As there was no anaesthetic to knock out the patient he'd be given buckets of booze before the surgeon got to work with his saw. Afterwards his remaining 'stump' would be dipped in tar to protect it.

Some shipboard surgeons would also slap a handful of maggots on pirates' wounds because they only gobbled up the rotting flesh and the bacteria, leaving the healthy flesh untouched.

NB: Don't try this at home. It's only special sorts of maggots that do this (e.g. ones with medical qualifications, university degrees etc) and if you get the wrong sort, you'll end up being eaten alive.

Dampier's Daily Diary

May 1680: Somewhere off the coast of Ecuador: Good news! We have captured a Spanish ship with 3,276 pieces of eight on board. Bad news: Some of my buccaneer mates shot the ship's priest then chucked him overboard before he was dead. I wasn't too happy about that. (Come to think of it, I bet the priest wasn't either!)

Pieces of eight

A popular catchphrase with parrots and something that pirates loved to collect, pieces of eight were the coins that the Spanish minted from their hoards of stolen South American silver. They were called pieces of eight because each one was worth eight reales, which in today's money would come to about £20. So if you'd swiped a chest full of pieces of eight, you'd be feeling pretty pleased about it.

Pieces of eight were decorated with a scene

showing the two pillars of Hercules, said to stand at the gateway between the Old World (Europe) and the New World (America), and two half circles, which represented those two worlds. This image eventually metamorphosed into the $ dollar sign, used on American notes and coins today.

Dampier's Daily Diary
October 1680 Somewhere off the coast of Peru: We have been at sea for weeks now with hardly any food or water. I am swollen up and my mouth is full of blood and pus. Yes, I've got the dreaded scurvy. I fear I will soon die.

DISGUSTING DISEASES — SCURVY

CAUSES: Not eating enough fruit and green vegetables. Not getting enough vitamin C.

Pirates were often at sea for yonks, so supplies of fresh fruit and veg always ran out or rotted ages before they reached their destination. Most pirates also preferred to only eat 'manly' meat, rather than namby-pamby peas and soppy sprouts.

65

SYMPTOMS: a) You feel miserable, tired and totally lacking in get-up-and-go.

b) Your skin goes pale and you get big blue blotches all over your body.

c) You become bloated like a balloon and your vision goes blurred.

d) Your gums go all spongy and droopy and begin to drip blood and pus. Then all your teeth fall out.

e) You get diarrhoea.

f) Old wounds reopen, then you begin to rot!

g) And finally … you die.

TREATMENT: Eat lots of fresh fruit (especially citrus fruit) and vegetables.

EAT YOUR VEGETABLES OR YOU'LL GROW UP ALL BLOATED AND BLOTCHY LIKE THE CAPTAIN.

A British doctor eventually discovered that eating plenty of citrus fruits such as limes, oranges and lemons cured scurvy, so the Royal Navy began giving rations of lime juice to its sailors. And that's why British people are sometimes referred to as 'Limeys'.

Dampier's Daily Diary

28 October 1680: Took over a Spanish town today. Stole all their vegetables and fruit and ate the lot. Feeling loads better!

30 January 1681: Somewhere off the coast of Chile: Very hot today and also a terrible disaster. Ninety of our buccaneers attacked Arica town but were chased off down the beach by Spanish cavalry. Luckily for our shipmates, the big boulders on the beach slowed their horses down. But Spaniards on the cliff tops began dropping rocks on our men and squashing them. The survivors hid out in caves but became so parched by the heat that they ended up having to drink their own wee to survive. Only 45 have made it back alive. Our leader, Captain Watling, is also dead. The Spanish chopped off his head and paraded it around their town on the end of a stick.

1682: We are in Virginia, America - a great place for us buccaneers to chill without fear of arrest. Everywhere I go I see black slaves working in the tobacco fields all a day long without a penny for their labour. I have a painful red swelling on my leg which I put a plaster on.

When I took it off there was a little tube poking out of the swelling. The lady I'm staying with thought it was one of my nerves sticking out. But I know it isn't. It's a guinea worm!

YOO HOO

DISGUSTING DISEASES — GUINEA WORMS
(AKA FIERY SERPENTS)

CAUSE: Drinking water containing water fleas that contain guinea-worm larvae. Your stomach acids kill the fleas but not the worms so they grow up inside your body, becoming a metre long in just one year. The boy guinea worms die while the lady guinea worms, full to bursting with babies, wriggle their way to a spot just under the surface of your skin, where they give birth. All the baby worms wriggle about too and soon a big painful swelling appears on your skin, which eventually breaks open. At this point Mrs Guinea Worm sticks out her head and all her little ones go rushing into the big wide world outside. Which is probably water, because by now you are in so much pain that you are more than likely soothing your leg in a stream, pond or bucket. The baby guinea worms now get swallowed by water fleas who get swallowed by unsuspecting thirsty humans and yes … here we go again!

Dampier's Daily Diary
Uuurgh! Every day I wrap my guinea worm around a stick and pull a bit more out.

A few weeks later: There is now about two feet of guinea worm hanging out of my leg and it hurts like mad.

My friend was taking his poorly horse to see a black doctor today who is said to know magic cures, so I went with him. The doctor waved his hands over the horse's sore, put special powder on it and said strange words. So I asked him if he'd do the same to my guinea worm. He did, and charged me one white cockerel for the treatment.

3 days later: Hurrah! I am cured. My guinea worm is gone. My friend's horse is better too! Is that amazing, or what?

23 August 1683: At sea again, we have been blasted along by a hurricane for three days now. All our sails are down!

24 August: Nearly lost it today. Ship turned broadside on to massive waves and it looked like we would certainly capsize. And we couldn't raise

the sails as the wind would have ripped them to shreds. So me and another chap climbed the mast. When we were halfway up, we stopped and spread out our coat tails to catch the wind. It worked! We turned into the wind again!

William's last awfully big adventure

William went on lots more hair-raising buccaneering expeditions, spending his time between trips writing his travel best-sellers. Then, in 1708, at the ancient age of 56, he got itchy feet, yet again! So he teamed up with a 29-year-old sea captain called Woodes Rogers and went off pirating for the last time. Handily for the two swashbucklers, Britain was at war with France and Spain (yes, again!) so they were able to say they were privateers, rather than nasty common pirates.

Privateers

Privateers were pirates who were given a licence (also called a letter of marque) by their governments, which allowed them to attack ships belonging to enemies of their country, without fear of being prosecuted for it. In times of war, this saved governments money because they didn't have to spend quite so much on building up their navies. However, when wars finished, many privateers went back to being pirates, attacking ships of all nations, willy-nilly (which annoyed Mr Nilly no end).

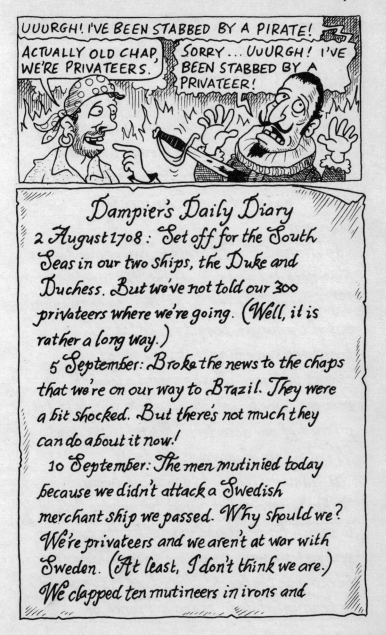

Dampier's Daily Diary

2 August 1708: Set off for the South Seas in our two ships, the Duke and Duchess. But we've not told our 300 privateers where we're going. (Well, it is rather a long way.)

5 September: Broke the news to the chaps that we're on our way to Brazil. They were a bit shocked. But there's not much they can do about it now!

10 September: The men mutinied today because we didn't attack a Swedish merchant ship we passed. Why should we? We're privateers and we aren't at war with Sweden. (At least, I don't think we are.) We clapped ten mutineers in irons and

whipped a load more. What a revolting rabble these common seamen are! Why can't they just do as they're told?

14 November : After 14 weeks at sea we have finally landed in Brazil. I immediately went turtle hunting, even though a massive tornado with sheet lightning was sweeping the coast. I had no choice. Everyone was starving!

19 November : Morning: Two of our sailors have deserted and run off into the jungle. Afternoon: They're back! They came running out of the jungle, begging to be taken back on board and screaming that they were being chased by tigers. Next moment a load of baboons came bouncing out of the jungle in hot pursuit of our deserters. Tigers! I ask you! What a pair of ignorant thickwits!

31 January 1709 : Huge shock today. When we arrived at Juan Fernandez Island to search for fruit and vegetables (to cure our scurvy), we were surprised to see a huge fire burning on the beach! The island is supposed to be uninhabited. Fearing French or

Spanish soldiers had got here before us we sent a party of armed men ashore.

Moments later, a hairy ape-man came running out of the woods screaming at them like a lunatic and frantically waving a white rag. Gibbering wildly, he kept shouting something that sounded like, 'moron', or 'moon'. When the men brought this creature to me, I could hardly believe my eyes! Underneath that huge great beard was Alexander Selkirk! The chap Captain Stradling marooned here more than four years ago! By some miracle he has survived!

Castaway

Alexander had been a crew member on one of William's earlier buccaneering expeditions. But he had fallen out with his ship's captain and been marooned. Astonishingly, Alexander had not only survived his four year and four month desert-island dumping, but he'd actually thrived on it! When William and his sick sea-mates staggered ashore, it was Alexander who looked after them, feeding them up on goat meat, stewed seal, turnips and cabbage.

Pirates often marooned their own mates on deserted islands as a punishment, or dumped their victims there, just to get them out of the way. When pirates marooned a mate, they usually left him a gun to kill himself with – because being left all alone was considered to be a fate worse than death.

However, Alexander proved that it is possible to survive being marooned. So just in case you find yourself all alone on a deserted tropical island, here's a guide to…

Surviving marooning the Alexander Selkirk way
Problem: Being eaten alive by rats. Whenever Alexander went to sleep rats gnawed his hands and feet.
Solution: He made friends with the island's wild cats and soon had his own posse of pussies protecting his tootsies from the rats.

Problem: Finding food and shelter on the beach.
Solution: Alexander set up home in a cave and caught shellfish. But the beach was invaded by hordes of ferocious sea lions so he had to move inland.

Problem: Finding food inland.
Solution: He found plenty to eat, including wild turnips and goats, which he shot with his musket (the goats, not

the turnips). By the time his ammunition ran out he'd become so fit that he was able to outrun the goats and kill them with his knife (after flooring them with a flying rugby-tackle).

Problem: Worn tools.
Solution: Alexander made new knife blades from barrel hoops he found washed up on the beach by beating the metal into shape with stones.

Problem: Making a shelter.
Solution: Alexander built two wooden huts, which he lined with goat skins to make them extra snug.

Problem: Loneliness and boredom.
Solution: Alexander read his Bible and sang hymns. He also 'kidnapped' some baby goats and brought them up as pets. He also sang and danced with them and his cats.

Problem: What to wear?
Solution: Alexander unravelled his socks for thread then used an old nail to sew himself a new goatskin jacket, trousers and cap. His feet became as tough as old boots from walking barefoot on the volcanic island rock.

Dampier's Daily Diary

7 June 1709: We have arrived at Gorgona Island where there is plenty of food, wood and water. I have told the men to eat monkeys and baboons because I have never tasted anything so delicious.

> MMM, FISH 'N CHIMPS, MY FAVOURITE!

12 June: The other day the men caught a sloth in the jungle and brought it on board. It climbed the ship's mast very very slowly! I timed it. It took a whole two hours to get to the top!

> COME ON, LIGHTNING!

In readiness for attacking the Spanish, Captain Rogers has had everyone fighting each other in a pretend battle. We even had the surgeons doing mock operations on 'wounded' men covered in false blood made from red lead and water.

November 1709: We are once more terribly low on food. So low that that our ship's steward goes to bed with the storehouse keys tied to his willy. The other night a starving crew member managed to steal the keys without waking him and helped himself to bread and sugar. However, he wasn't so nifty at reattaching them and was caught and punished!

21 December 1710: We have sighted our prize. We will attack at dawn.

December 22nd 1710 - After a short and fierce battle we have taken a Spanish galleon. Captain Rogers was hit in the jaw with musket shot.

OW!

March 1710: Food almost gone. The men catch the rats which scurry about our ship then sell them for sixpence each. They are eaten with great gusto!

RAT ON A STICK!

June 1710: One of the men jumped in the sea for a swim today. We had warned him not to but he took no notice. Minutes later, a huge shark seized him in its jaws and bit him in two!

October 1710: We reached home today. Things in London have changed so! For instance, the new St Paul's Cathedral is now finished. What a magnificent building it is. We have plunder and treasure worth £150,000*. I think I may ease off the privateering now. It's so exhausting!

William died in 1715 aged 63, worn out by his non-stop adventuring.

* £15,000,000 in today's money.

LIFE AS A PIRATE – HARDSHIP, HARDSHIP, HARDSHIP! (...AND SOME HARD SHIPS)

It's amazing that William survived to the ripe old age of 63. Life as a pirate was generally a savage struggle for survival, which many pirates lost after just a few months or years at sea.

Just so *you* don't get any silly ideas about going off pirating, here's a taste of sort of the sort of hardships, and hard ships, sea rovers had to put up with and sail in. Welcome to the stinking, damp, leaky, creaky, cramped, dangerous, nauseating roller-coaster that is going to be your home for the next few months – that's if you don't sink, get blown to pieces, drown, get eaten by sharks, die from the bloody flux, get stabbed to death or marooned, etc. etc. etc.

Sardines

Overcrowding: cramped pirate ships always carried more crew than they were built for because they had to outnumber their intended victims. So, on a boat 40 metres long and 12 metres wide, there would often be as many as 250 smelly, bad-tempered pirates, all squidged together as they tried to work, sleep, play and slay.

THERE'S NOT ENOUGH ROOM TO SWING A CAT IN HERE!

WELL, THAT'S ONE GOOD THING!

Deck soup

Pirates had lots of bad habits, including spitting, which everyone (apart from Premier League footballers) knows is a very unpleasant and unhygienic habit. And because pirates had rotten teeth and gums and chronic catarrh (due to the damp conditions they lived in) their saliva was spectacularly putrid and colourful. This spit would mix with the rainwater on the decks and then ferment, turning into a disgusting toxic soup that sloshed around the ship as it swayed this way and that. Regular sailors in the merchant and Royal navies scrubbed their decks every day with pumice stone and sand, then washed them down with vinegar and salt water. However, pirates, being lazy good-for-nothings, would be content to splash around in the gloop. Very occasionally, if they'd happened to pinch more brandy than they could possible guzzle in a month of fundays, they'd sloosh that around the decks to disinfect them.

A drop in the ocean

Toilets? Forget it! There aren't any. If you want a wee you walk out on to an overhanging platform and tiddle in the sea. But, before you do, make sure you check which way the wind's blowing.

If you need to sit down to relieve yourself you must go to the bow of your boat then balance precariously above the sea on a plank with holes cut in it.

NOW, PLEASE DON'T WASH YOUR HANDS

WELL, WE ARE PIRATES

The well-dressed pirate

TROPICAL KIT: NO CLOTHES AT ALL

HAIR PULLED BACK TIGHT AND HELD IN PLACE BY PIRATE HAIR GEL (A DOLLOP OF TAR)

BIG WOOLLEN SHIRT WITH BELT

GOLD EARRING - LOOKED COOL, ALSO USED TO PAY FOR BURIAL COSTS WHEN PIRATE POPPED CLOGS

TROUSERS AKA SLOPPERS MADE FROM OLD SAILS

CLOTHES ALL PLASTERED WITH TAR SO THEY WERE WATERPROOF, LASTED LONGER AND REPELLED SWORD CUTS

BARE FEET TO GET A BETTER GRIP ON WET DECKS AND RIGGING

UNDIES? YOU MUST BE JOKING!

CLOTHES WERE PERMANENTLY DAMP, SMELLY AND ITCHY

Weather

You'll be so frozen and soaked by winter storms that your skin will turn blue, you'll shake from head to toe and feel as if you'll never be dry or warm again. And, at night, when the seas are raging, the wind is screaming and waves are bigger than small skyscrapers, you'll be expected to climb hundreds of metres into the rigging in pitch blackness, hanging on with one frozen hand, while you use the other to make life-or-death adjustments to the sails, which will be flapping and whipping like gigantic ghosts. One slip and you'll be hurled into the icy seas or smashed on to the decks, breaking all the bones in your body. You'll also be grilled by tropical sun, which beats down on you day after day, turning your skin the colour and texture of old boots and making your tongue feel like a 100-year-old flip-flop.

Sleeping

When the weather is stormy, cold or wet, you'll sleep on the inside 'forecastle decks' with the hatches closed to stop seawater pouring in. This means you'll be 'cheek' by jowl with dozens of snoring, sweaty, unwashed pirates. In addition to their industrial-strength BO, you'll be breathing in their chronic bad breath, not to mention the pongy gases that explode from their personal plumbing systems at regular, noisy intervals. If you're lucky, you may have a hammock to sleep in, so as your ship lurches and tosses on the high seas, you'll remain more or less stable. But more likely, you'll be rocking and rolling on hard, damp and mouldy ship's timbers, as mice, rats, cockroaches and fleas energetically investigate all your nooks and crannies. And remember, if you suddenly need to get up in the night, your headroom is a bit limited. When the weather's good and the seas are calmer, sensible pirates sleep on the open decks or curl up aloft in the folded sails.

The bilges

The bilges are at the very bottom of your boat. They quickly fill up with slimy water, rotten fish and meat, decaying fruit and vegetables, and human waste. The air down there eventually becomes so poisonous that it's

WELL, I RATHER LIKE IT DOWN HERE!

impossible to breathe. Nevertheless, you must take turns working the bilge pumps, which have to be operated almost constantly if you want to stay afloat. The bilges are also home to verminous horrors such as cockroaches, rats and maggots.

Pirate quality time – things to do on board

• Mend your clothes: Your clothes would be forever getting torn and worn and, as pirates usually had just one outfit, they had to do running repairs.

• Get drunk: Boozing was probably the most popular pirate pastime of all, with many pirates remaining more or less pickled for most of their adult lives.

• Play games like cards, backgammon, dice… (trivial pursuit, deadly pursuit): Like many lazy good-for-nothing wastes of space, pirates loved to fritter away their time and ill-gotten gains by gambling for hours on end.

• Listen to the band: As it was so hard to tune in to local pirate radio stations, many pirate ships had their own live music in the form of a band (which they'd more than likely nicked from another ship).

• Act out little plays: Yes, they really did. These were often courtroom dramas in which one pirate pretended to be a judge, sentencing the others to all manner of horrible punishments. For pirates, who lived in constant fear of being caught and hanged, it would be a little bit of drama therapy. (Rather like a bad dream you know you can wake up from.) However, at one of these little shows, one pirate gave such a convincing performance as the judge that one of his shipmates (who obviously wasn't the sharpest sword in the weapons cupboard) became convinced it was all for real. Fearing for his life, he threw a bomb at the 'jury' and chopped off the judge's arm with his cutlass. (Just think – if he'd chopped off his thumbs they could have called him Justice Fingers! Ha!)

• Look after your pets: Like lots of sailors, pirates had pets like cats and dogs, and also made pets of the animals they managed to capture while they were wandering around faraway places. Parrots were the most popular exotic pet, but pirates also kept monkeys. One pirate even had a pet penguin!

Pirate quality time – things to get up to in port
Can't tell you that – you're far too young!

The ships (hard and otherwise)
Pirates didn't go to the trouble of saving up for a nice ship to go sea-roving in. They simply pinched whatever they fancied, then gave it a maritime makeover to suit their needs.

The pirates' favourite ships were sloops and schooners because they were nippy and nimble and could be sailed into shallow water where big warships couldn't reach them.

Baddy boats
Schooner

The name of this ship comes from an American word, 'scoon', which means to skim along the water. Most schooners had two masts and could carry 75 pirates, eight cannon and four swivel guns. Many schooners were able to navigate water as shallow as 2 metres. This meant they could hide in bays and coves as they waited to ambush passing merchant ships. They were ideally suited to the 'hit-and-run' tactics of pirates.

Sloop

Sloops were popular with both smugglers and pirates, and were even nippier and nimbler than schooners. A single-masted sloop could travel at 11 knots (about 11 miles an hour) and was quite easy to manoeuvre in shallow channels. Sloops also made excellent 'hit-and-run' ships.

Brigantine

Brigantines were more suited to proper ship-against-ship sea battles, as opposed to hit-and-run raids. Pirate fleet captains would often choose to be on board a brigantine if they knew they were going have to take on the big guns of the Royal Navy. They could carry at least ten cannon and about 100 pirates. They also had twice as much cargo space as a sloop.

Square rigger

These really big ships weren't nearly as manoeuvrable as sloops, schooners and brigantines. However, weighing in at 350 tonnes, they were three times the size of schooners, really scary-looking, and ideal for long voyages and transporting loot. They could carry as many as 200 pirates and more than 20 cannon, and were chosen by pirate captains as the flagships for their fleets.

Goody Boats
Galleon

The Spanish treasure fleets were made up of these massive three-masted, three-decked ships. They were slow but well defended with heavy cannon, so pirates treated them with respect when they were attacking them.

Merchantman

These large three-masted passenger-and-cargo ships had a crew of about 20 sailors. It usually took them about four weeks to sail from England to America. They could carry as many as 16 cannon, but if pirates attacked them their crews were far too small to handle them so they usually surrendered.

East Indiaman

These cargo ships were twice the size of square-riggers and were built to carry phenomenally valuable cargoes from the Far East to Europe. If pirates captured an East Indiaman they knew they'd hit the jackpot.

Man-of-war

These were the 1,000-tonne, three-masted monsters of the Spanish, English and French navies. They carried more than 60 cannon and pirates knew that taking them on was a complete no-brainer. So they usually stayed well out of their way, hiding from them in shallow bays and coves.

A PIRATE SCHOONER

HEAD (THE LOO)

FOREMAST

SAILS

CAPSTAN - FOR HOISTING HEAVY THINGS ABOARD

CANNON

OOPS!

ANCHOR: SO YOU CAN STOP MID-OCEAN

HULL

BALLAST (TO KEEP THE SHIP STABLE) INCLUDED: BARRELS OF WATER / ROCKS / SPARE GUN BARRELS

BARNACLES AND TEREDO WORMS

BUCKET OF SAND: IN CASE OF FIRE (QUITE LIKELY IN ROUGH WEATHER)

'GALLEY' (KITCHEN IN LANDLUBBER SPEAK): BUILT OF BRICK AND IRON WELL AWAY FROM GUNPOWDER STORE

MAIN MAST

RIGGING

CAPTAIN'S CABIN:
AT THE STERN,
AWAY FROM THE
WORST WEATHER—
EASILY DEFENDED
IN ATTACK OR
MUTINY

CREW'S
SLEEPING
SPACE
BELOW
DECKS

BLERG!

THE
TILLER

POWDER
MAGAZINE

STORE ROOM
FOR CHARTS
AND TREASURE

THE
RUDDER
FOR
STEERING

CAPTAIN KIDD AND HIS BLOODY BUCKET 1645-1701

Captain William Kidd was a big, stroppy Scotsman who wore a shoulder-length wig and really groovy clothes (well, groovy for the 1600s).

YOU LAUGHING AT MY THREADS?

He was also a bully who would thrash the living daylights out of any members of his crew who upset him. He was born in the seaport of Dundee in Scotland. When he was five, his sea-captain father died, leaving Mrs Kidd to scrape by on very little money. Some years later, just after his mum had re-married, William ran away to sea. Hardly anything is known about his early years as a sailor. However, by the time he'd reached the ripe old age of 44, he'd become a privateer, warring against the French in the Caribbean. And that's where our shocking story of double-crossing, disaster and death begins!

One day, Captain's Kidd's crew decided they'd rather be pirates than privateers, so they pinched his ship while he was ashore and, led by a seaman called Robert Culliford, they sailed off without him.

After this, he went to New York, having heard that his crew had fled there with his ship. He didn't find his ship but he did arrive just as some English and Dutch bigwigs were having a war about who should be in charge of the American city. Captain Kidd helped one lot win the squabble and they loved him to bits for it.

Not long after this he married a rich widow and became one of the wealthiest men in town. However, after a few years, he became bored with being rich and married, and went off to London to hatch a plot with a couple of devious wheeler-dealers called Robert Livingston and Richard Coote. This is what they agreed:

Captain Kidd's Chronicles

25 February 1696: Sailed out of London docks today on my new ship, the 'Adventure Galley'. It weighs a whopping 300 tons and has 34 huge cannon. Those pirates and Frenchmen will quake in their boots when they see us! We're bound to catch hundreds of them. At Greenwich we passed the King's yacht. We were supposed to dip our flags to show respect. But I couldn't be bothered. Next minute, they fired a warning shot across our bows. But I still wasn't bothered. I simply sailed past them while my men up in the rigging took down their trousers and slapped their bare bottoms at them. Ha! What a jolly jape that was!

THE CHEEK OF IT!

January 1697: Not caught any pirates yet. Nor seen any French. But we've stopped off at Madagascar, every pirate's favourite resting place. There's bound to be a few pirate ships turn up sooner or later. Some of my crew have the scurvy too, so they need to cure themselves with fruit.

February 1697 : Just leaving Madagascar. Would you believe it? We were there a whole month and didn't see a single pirate ship! So, still no pirates or Frenchmen. And we're supposed to be back with the loot in a few weeks. Oh calamity!

April 1697: Our deadline passed weeks ago. But we've still not seen any pirates or Frenchmen! And now, to make matters worse, sea worms are gobbling our hull up. So we've stopped off at the lovely Maldives Islands for a wee bit of careening.

Careening

Pirates had to 'careen' the hulls of their ships at least three times a year. All manner of crud and gunge, including barnacles and seaweed, got stuck to the woodwork, causing it to fall apart. The warm waters of the Tropics are also home to all sorts of parasitic nasties known as teredo worms, which are rather partial to wooden ships and can nibble through the hull in no time.

MUNCH MUNCH

NOT BAD, BUT I PREFERRED HENRY MORGAN'S HULL.

How to careen your pirate ship

1 Find a secluded beach where you aren't likely to be taken by surprise and set upon by your enemies e.g. the Royal Navy, the Spanish Navy, French Navy and other pirates.

2 Drag your ship right up on to the beach, then unload it.

3 Set up a fortified camp because you're going to be here for a few days. Use old sails to make tents. Take the opportunity to get fresh water supplies, collect fruit and go hunting for fresh meat.

4 Tilt your ship to about 45 degrees using ropes and wooden poles to stop it from going all the way over – you wouldn't want that now, would you!

5 Hammer and scrape off all the crud and whatnot from your hull, e.g. barnacles, sea worms and seaweed.

TIP: the best way to get rid of barnacles is to burn the blighters – just the barnacles though.

6 Replace any completely rotten planks.

7 'Caulk' the gaps between the planks by forcing them open with an iron wedge then stuffing them with oakum (bits of rope fibre covered with tar). Tap the oakum in tight with a mallet and caulking iron.

8 Coat all the woodwork with a mixture of tar, tallow and sulphur.

If you do not careen:

a) Your ship will become slow and hard to manoeuvre.

b) Other pirates will point at your ship and go…

TUT TUT! WOULD YOU LOOK AT THE STATE OF THAT!

c) Finally, large holes will appear in your woodwork and you will sink.

NB: One of these might not be true.

Tip: Before you go off pirating again, remember to put your ship upright.

> *Captain Kidd's Chronicles*
> *August 1697: Stopped the 'Mary', a square-rigged two-master. While its Captain, Thomas Parker and I were in my cabin, my gunner, William Moore (a real pain in the arsenal!), took a boarding party on to the 'Mary' and stole five bales of coffee, 60 pounds of pepper, some myrrh, navigation instruments, clothes, rice, plumblines and eight firearms. But that's not all! Next they strung up the Indian crew and began cruelly striking them with*

their cutlasses to make them reveal where they'd hidden their valuables.

PS I have decided to kidnap Captain Parker and his officer, Antonio. I wonder? Does this make me a pirate, too?

3 September 1697: Arrived at Carwar. Nine of my crew deserted while we were loading wood and water. When the authorities there asked me if I'd kidnapped Parker and Antonio, I was indignant and told them I had not. But all the time I was acting the innocent, I had the two of them locked in the hold of the Adventure Galley! Ha ha! I am really getting to be a rogue, me thinks!

PS Still not caught any pirate ships or seen any French.

22 September 1697: Chased by two Portuguese warships. Blasted the smaller one with our cannon but fled when the big one turned up.

30 October 1697: Bit of trouble today. We spotted a Dutch merchant ship and my crew were all for attacking it. But I said, 'No!' Not long afterwards, that trouble-making gunner, William Moore

(yes, him again) said to me, 'You have brought us to ruin. We are desolate.'

The cheeky scoundrel! I was overcome with rage!

'I have not brought you to ruin!' I roared. 'I have not done an ill thing to ruin you. You are a dog to give me those words.'

Then, just to make entirely sure he knew who his master was, I hit him on the head with a wooden bucket. He went out like a light!

PS Still not caught any pirate ships.

31 October 1697 Uh oh! More trouble. Or should that be 'Moore' trouble. Yes, yesterday William Moore nutted the bucket and today he's kicked it. He's dead! Apparently I hit him so hard I broke his skull! No wonder he went so ... pail!

30 January 1698: Hurrah! We've finally taken our prize! The 350-tonner 'Quedah Merchant', loaded with 1,200 bales of fabric, 1,400 bags of brown sugar, 84 bales of silk, 80 chests of opium, iron, saltpetre and more!

Apparently it belongs to the Great Moghul of India. ——→ But more to the point, we've stolen about £50,000* worth of booty! And here's the best news. When I went in the captain's cabin, I found a big wooden chest. I made sure no one else was around, then broke open the padlocks and lifted the lid. It was overflowing with all manner of treasure: enormous diamonds, silver rings, rubies, emeralds, gold nuggets, all sorts! I've hidden it all now (I don't think I'll mention it to anyone else).

Spring 1698: My Adventure Galley is in a poorly way. The worms have eaten through the hull. The only thing that is stopping us falling apart are the ropes we've wrapped all the way around her. I've got eight men operating the bilge pumps, too. Our only hope is to try and reach Madagascar again.

April 1698: Have finally arrived at Madagascar, still more or less in one piece. Phew!

* About five million pounds in today's money.

PIRATE PARADISES: MADAGASCAR

THE HUGE TROPICAL PARADISE ISLAND OF MADAGASCAR — TWICE THE SIZE OF BRITAIN

NB: NO INTERFERING EUROPEAN OFFICIALS — I.E. NO LAW AND ORDER DO EXACTLY AS YOU PLEASE WITHOUT FEAR OF BEING ARRESTED!

GORGEOUS WEATHER

STUNNING SCENERY

SERIOUS CHILLING

SECLUDED BAYS AND SANDY BEACHES, PERFECT FOR SHIP CLEANING

INDIAN OCEAN → ← AFRICA 250 MILES YOUR VICTIMS ARE ONLY A SHORT TRIP AWAY! MERCHANT SHIPS LOADED WITH GOODIES!

WONDERFUL WILDLIFE

ONCE YOU'VE VISITED MADAGASCAR YOU'LL FIND IT HARD TO LEAVE AND TO PROVE A POINT, WE'VE ALREADY GOT OVER 1,500 PIRATES LIVING HERE, THEY'VE SETTLED AND MARRIED LOCAL GIRLS.

Captain Kidd's Chronicles

April 1698: I don't believe it! Guess who is also here in Madagascar? Only that rotter Robert Culliford! The knave who stole my ship all those years ago. I'd like to settle my accounts with him but we are outnumbered by his pirate gang and my men aren't keen anyway.

May 1698: Oh disaster! 96 of my men have deserted to Culliford. I am now barricaded in my cabin with my treasure and they are trying to get in. But I am well prepared for them. I have 40 small arms and 24 pistols laid in front of me, all loaded and ready.

Back home things were also getting a bit tricky for Captain Kidd. When the Great Moghul of India discovered that his treasure had been stolen by Captain Kidd, he was furious. And he let the British government know. That made *them* really furious because they and their business partners, the East India Company, had been making a fortune out of the Moghul and the Indian people. So, in order to keep the Moghul happy, they declared Captain Kidd a common pirate who was to be hunted down and brought to justice.

Meanwhile, Captain Kidd had managed to escape from Madagascar and was making his way back to America with his treasure and what was left of his crew. But he didn't know he'd been declared a pirate. So when he arrived home, he got a shock when was arrested by Coote, the very person who had sent him off on his adventure in the first place.

Coote sent him back to England where he was locked up in the dreadful hell-hole known as Newgate Prison, to await his trial for piracy and the bucket-murder of William Moore.

Ten good reasons not to get put in Newgate prison

1 Having been rebuilt after the Great Fire of London, Newgate Prison looks very impressive from outside, with its four statues representing liberty, truth, justice and mercy. Ha! Don't be fooled. Inside you'll find only cruelty, corruption, violence and sickness.

2 It's crawling with cockroaches, rats and fleas and oozing with disgusting stinking filth. Everywhere you look there are steaming, unemptied toilet pots surrounded by thousands of buzzing bluebottles. The stench will make you sick.

3 You'll be banged up with the most evil, filthy, crazy, degenerate, dangerous and diseased criminals in the land ... three to a bed! And by the way, you'll have to pay a daily rent for the 'privilege' of sharing your cell with these creatures who are going to make what's left of your life hell!

4 You'll also be keeping company with hens, pigs, chickens, dogs and cats. And no one bothers to clear up after them.

5 Just like you, lots of the inmates are condemned to death. So they don't care how they behave. Anything goes. Well, they've nothing to lose, have they?

6 There are no proper windows or ventilation in Newgate. So in addition to the sickening stink, you'll be in complete darkness. The only way to see your way around is with candles. But they're also a 'privilege', i.e. you have to pay for them too.

7 And while we're on the subject of money, when you arrive you'll be met by some very nasty individuals who will tell you to 'Strip or pay!' In other words, if you want to keep your clothes, then yes, you must hand over money for this 'privilege'.

8 Just to make sure there's plenty of drunkenness and lots of the violent, chaotic behaviour that always accompanies it, Newgate has its own 'in-clink' pub. But of course, you'll also have to pay to drown your sorrows.

9 It's a good idea to plead guilty or not guilty to your crimes. If you refuse to plead, you'll be taken into the 'pressing' yard where you'll have large stones piled on top of you, with more being added each day until a plea is finally 'squeezed' out of you.

10 Before you finally appear before the courts, like all prisoners, you'll be stripped and washed all over with vinegar.

Captain Kidd's Chronicles

April 1699: I was brought to Newgate prison today. This place is worse than Hell. The stink is sickening. Compared to it, the fetid bilges of a pirate ship are a rose-scented country garden. As I entered the darkness, I felt a moving carpet crunching under my feet. Uuurgh! It's lice! The floors are thick with them.

16 May 1701: A grim day. I have been in this hellhole for two years now. It is my tenth wedding anniversary. I have not seen my dear wife and daughter for a year and a half. I fear I never will. This morning I heard the London mob roaring for some poor wretch to be executed so that they might enjoy his agony on the gallows.

Later: My appeal for mercy has been rejected. I am to die on 23 May.

22 May 1701: My death approaches fast. I tried my best not to be a pirate but things turned out all wrong. I wait in hope for a pardon.

SNIFF SOB

> *23 May 1701: It is the morning of my execution. No pardon has arrived. I am drinking large amounts of rum to quell the terror I feel inside. Myself and nine other pirates are to be taken to the gallows at Execution Dock in three carts.*
>
> *I have given away my slave to the prison-keeper. Uuurp! farewell, cruel world!*

So that was it. William was to be taken to Execution Dock in Wapping, the place on the banks of the River Thames specially set aside for the execution of pirates.

The Wapping (Great Newspaper!)
BAD NOOSE - GOOD NOOSE!
CAPTAIN KIDD HANGED - TWICE!

Today I witnessed the hanging of the notorious pirate, Captain Kidd. What a drama it was! It felt like every beggar, thief, workman's apprentice, lady-of-the-night and cut-throat in London had turned up to see this former much-respected gentleman dance the hempen jig. As the three black-draped carts carrying the miserable trussed-up pirates forced their way through the screaming mob, guttersnipes, up to their usual tricks, hurled poo-smeared dead cats and dogs into the crowd, while haggard, old crones mockingly cried out, 'Chuck us some treasure me dears! Pieces of eight! Pieces of eight!'

But I don't think Captain Kidd even heard them. He was sozzled! Pie-eyed! Three sheets to the wind! As were the stinking, wild-eyed rabble who guzzled cheap booze bought from the taverns and the baskets of the ale-wives.

After three miles and two hours, the carts finally reached Execution Dock. As the pirates were led to the gallows at the river's edge, street urchins crawled through the legs of people and horses so they might shake hands with the tragic Captain Kidd before he died.

The mob went mad now, yelling, 'Tell us where you hid your treasure, Captain Kidd!' surging forward, only to

be beaten back by mounted guards.

'Beware of false promises made by greedy men!' yelled Kidd. 'I am innocent!'

And then, just as the executions were about to take place, six pardons arrived. Alas, none were for Kidd. So, as the freed men wept tears of joy, nooses were placed around the necks of Kidd and the others. Then, as the clocks of London struck six, the hangmen knocked away the blocks. The crowd roared, three men danced on the end of a rope, turned purple, wet themselves, and died. But not Kidd! His rope had broken! So he was hanged again. And, as the sun set over the Thames, he finally died.

After the pirates had been hanged, their bodies were tied to posts on the riverbank so that they disappeared under the murky incoming tide water, only to reappear as it went out. After this had happened three times, they were cut down and Captain Kidd's body was taken to Tilbury point, where it was dipped in tar, then put in a specially made cage which was dangled from a gibbet post. For years to come, all sailors entering and leaving the port of London would see his rotting remains hanging there and be reminded that being a pirate often leads to a very unpleasant end.

Note: No one is actually sure what happened to all the gold and silver Captain Kidd kept secret from the other pirates. Treasure hunters have spent years trying to find it, but with no luck. However, during the course of the research for this book, the author was fortunate enough to come across a coded treasure map, believed to have been drawn by Captain Kidd's old friend, Leonardo da Vinci. For further details, please turn to the bonus, 'This-is-where-Captain-Kidd's-treasure-is-buried' diagram on page 563.

BLACK BART AND HIS RECORD-BREAKING REIGN OF TERROR
1682–1722

Some pirates – like Henry Morgan, Blackbeard and Anne Bonny – actually wanted to be pirates. But others – like Bartholomew Roberts – only began their nautical naughtiness after being taken prisoner by pirates and 'volunteered' into the swashbuckling life by their captors. Nevertheless, Bartholomew took to pirating like a (killer) duck to water, eventually becoming the number-one, high-seas hyper-hooligan, hugely out-plundering every pirate who'd ever lived. During his three-year reign of fear, he and his 200-strong posse broke all pirating records, capturing more than 400 ships and stealing enough loot and treasure to keep them all in designer eye-patches and turbocharged bilge pumps for the rest of their lives.

Bartholomew was born in Wales in 1682. Apart from that, hardly anything is known about his early life. However, we do know he began his seafaring career working on slave-ships and soon became an expert in all things relating to ships and the sea. In June 1719, his ship was boarded by pirates and he and the rest of the crew were taken prisoner. Shortly after this, the pirates' leader, Howell Davis (who also happened to be Welsh) was killed. Realizing that Bart was a very tough man and an expert sailor (not to mention Welsh), they immediately elected him to be their new captain.

Not long after being elected Captain, Bartholomew changed his name to the much scarier-sounding Black Bart (having decided that 'Beige Bart' didn't have quite the same bloodcurdling ring to it). By the time Bart was a 30-something, he was said to be 'pistol-proof'. This is the pirate way of saying that someone is expert at controlling their men, fighting battles at sea and handling their ship.

In his new role as a buccaneer boss-man, Bart became fond of dressing up for big events such as sea battles and boarding parties (his favourite outfit being that of a swashbuckling pirate captain, rather than a nurse or traffic warden). So, resplendent in his crimson cuthroat's outfit, Bart became the

112

scourge of the seven seas – blasting here, torching there, and looting absolutely everywhere! In fact, he did so much burning, shooting, killing and looting that it would take a book the size of Bristol to record it all. So instead, here's a carefully chosen selection of…

BLACK BART'S GREATEST HITS (Part one)
(brought to you by Pirate Records)
· 1719: Principe Island, West Africa: Destroyed the town with our cannon. Plundered and sank two Portuguese ships. But this was just a warm-up for the real action. See below.
· 1719: Bahia, Brazil, South America: Them: Two forts, two men o' war, 32 well-armed ships, 1,000 men and 500 cannon. Us: One ship, 20 guns and 28 men (i.e. we were slightly outnumbered). The guys weren't for chancing it, but I says, 'Let's go get 'em!' So we went in, boarded the biggest, richest treasure ship in the harbour, fought like tigers, and won! Prize: masses of gold, diamonds, tobacco and more. We're buccaneering rich!*
· 1720: Trespassi, Newfoundland: Them: 22 ships, 1,000 men, hundreds of guns. Us: One ship, 12 guns and 160 men. We sailed in, black flags flying, drums beating and trumpets blasting. They surrendered without a fight. What a load of yellow-bellies! I had their captains whipped for being such baa lambs! Took over all the town and ships, stayed two weeks, terrorizing local folk, plundering everything we could lay hands on, and burning 26 ships and 150 fishing boats on the day we left. What a hoot that was!

---

* They were, too. In today's money, the plunder from this one attack was worth more than five million pounds.

· 1720: Dominica, Caribbean: Big Dutch war ship had the nerve to resist us. We beat 'em, then hung those Dutch dimwits from the yardarms, whipped 'em bloody, cut off the captain's ears and tortured the rest even worse than that! Prize: 14 ships! I am so BAD!

(To be continued...)

However, despite victories like these, everything didn't always go brilliantly for Bart and his boatloads of baddies. Wandering the world's vast oceans in a small leaky ship, being swept this way and that by unpredictable winds and killer currents, while using unreliable maps and the stars for guidance, was a *very* dangerous business. Every year, thousands of pirates and other seafarers died as their ships were bashed to bits by hurricanes, swallowed by raging seas, or simply lost in the endless oceans of the world, never to be seen again. Getting from one place to another was a huge challenge, requiring outstanding navigational and seafaring skills of the sort that made Bart the most successful pirate of his day. But sometimes, even *he* got it wrong!

Black Bart's Blog – Autumn 1720
All goes well. We've got a boatload of plunder and we're leaving the Caribbean for Africa. We'll put in at Sierra Leone and have some FUN!

Three weeks later: We've crossed the Atlantic and we're in sight of the Cape Verde Isles, off the African coast. We'll stop there for fresh water then continue on to Sierra Leone. But what's this I see? A couple of merchantmen on the horizon. Hmm, now there's an opportunity I can't ignore!

Later the same day: Bad decision! After attacking the merchantmen we've ended up further south west than I'd intended. It's gonna be tricky to make land now, especially with the strong wind blowing from the mainland. We'll have to try coming in again.

us

Island

Wind direction

Early evening same day: Suffering sea biscuits! We've missed again. We can see the island just a few leagues away, but we're being blown in the opposite direction. We'll just have to try once more.

Later that night: Blithering bilge pumps,

115

that didn't work either. And we can't even drop anchor now. The sea's far too deep!

Next morning: We are in BIG trouble! The winds are blowing us right back across the Atlantic to where we started from! And there's not a thing we can do about it! There's nothing between us and the Americas but thousands and thousands of miles of empty ocean.

Bad news flash! I've just been told we're down to the last barrel of water! So I've rationed it to one cupful a man each day. The nearest port is still six weeks away!

One week later: This is my worst nightmare come true! We're out in the Atlantic Deeps. Water almost gone. Rationed it to one mouthful a man a day. And still that wind blows.

Lost all track of time now. Some of the men became so desperately thirsty that they began drinking seawater. And now they've gone mad. Their screaming and gibbering is driving me insane, too.

The mad seawater-drinkers are dying like flies. We're throwing bodies into the sea every day.

Fog today! So we're hanging up cotton sheets to catch the moisture, ringing them out into buckets and drinking it.

Some poor wretches are drinking their own tiddle now. Yes, we're that desperate! But I must say they do seem a bit better for it.

The tiddle drinkers are dying now. It's been through them so many times it's turned completely poisonous.

Late December: Dozens dead! Water all gone. Food gone. I could murder a salmagundi! I dream of turtle soup all the time. We can't last. Sun beating down. My mouth feels like a buccaneer's armpit. But what's that in the sky?

Refreshment break

Running out of food and water like Bart and his lads did was one of a pirate's worst fears. So, before going on a long voyage, they would stock up with lots of drink and tack (pirate-speak for food). After all, they couldn't just pop into a port and do a really big shop, because if they did they might end up dancing the 'hempen jig'.

Tasty tack

• Food quickly went rotten, particularly in tropical areas, so pirate 'tack' often began the voyage in the freshest state possible.

• Pirates kept their hens alive for their cackle fruit (eggs in 'pirate').

• They also took preserved meat such as salted pork, smoked beef and dried cows' tongues.

• However, in the hot, humid, bacteria-rich atmosphere of the Tropics, even these would eventually rot.

• Pirates stopped off at quiet tropical islands to stock up on fresh meat. Many of the unsuspecting and tasty

118

animals who lived on these islands hadn't seen human beings before, so they were really easy to catch.

• Turtles were the pirates' favourite food. They'd sneak up on them while they were mating or laying eggs, then flip them on to their backs. Stowed in the holds of their ships, the live turtles could survive for up to six months without food or water. Pirates also bought fresh turtles at markets in places like Port Royal.

• Like many children, pirates weren't all that keen on eating fruit and vegetables, so they were probably quite pleased when their greengrocery supplies went rotten after just a few days at sea.

• Pirates also ate biscuits called hardtack or sea bread, made from flour, salt and water. The biscuits were baked four times which meant they would last for as long as five years. It also made it difficult for creepy-crawlies to nibble their way into them. But it also made them rock hard and almost impossible for humans to nibble their way into them either. However, in the damp Tropics, the biscuits soon went soft and became infested with tiny bread-beetle grubs, not to mention even bigger grubs, which ate the bread-beetle grubs. Most sensible swashbucklers tapped their hardtack so that all the grubs or beetles dropped out before they ate them (the biscuits, not the grubs and beetles).

119

• The most popular pirate nosh-up was salmagundi. The cook threw almost anything he could lay his hands on into the steep pot, mixed in lots of spices, then let it all bubble away for ages. The ingredients usually included turtle meat, fish, chicken, pork, beef, duck, pigeon, spiced wine, herbs, palm hearts, garlic, oil, hard-boiled eggs, anchovies, pickled onions, cabbage, grapes and olives.

Drink

Black Bart's favourite drink was tea. But most pirates preferred to guzzle alcohol. As Bart discovered, water supplies quickly became stagnant and slimy and usually ran out at the most inconvenient moments. And in those days of non-existent hygiene, you could never be sure that they were pure and free of the little nasties that caused horrible conditions like dysentery and guinea worm. Even water collected during stop-offs at idyllic tropical islands wasn't guaranteed to be free of tiny parasitic worms, bacteria and viruses.

The pirates' favourite types of booze were beer and rum. Their beer was kept in barrels or clay bottles, which were traditionally opened by a swift slash of the cutlass known as 'nicking'.

Rum was either drunk on its own or, more creatively, in the form of: Grog (rum and water), Bumboo (rum, sugar and nutmeg), Rumfustian (rum, raw eggs, sugar, sherry, gin and beer), Rumbullion (rum, wine, tea, lime juice, sugar and spices), Rumpsteak (rum with bits of meat floating in it). NB: One of these is not true.

120

Now, back to...

Bart's Blog

Late December 1720: Hurrah, it's a seagull! And that can only mean one thing. We must be near land.

A few hours later:

Land ahoy! Hurrah, we'll live to slay another day. Well, apart from all our mates who've died of thirst and hunger, we will. We're back in business! If I were a boozing man, I'd have a drink to celebrate.

Black Bart: rules (OK!)

Despite the fact that pirates have been scientifically proven to be 20 per cent human being and 80 per cent alcohol, Bart was a strict non-drinker who believed that boozing and buccaneering didn't mix. And he did his best to persuade his crew to cut down on *their* drinking too.

And it wasn't just their boozing he tried to regulate. Like many other pirate captains, Bart made up a list of 'articles' (rules and conditions) that were intended to make life amongst the bunch of cut-throats who made up his crew as disciplined and orderly as possible.

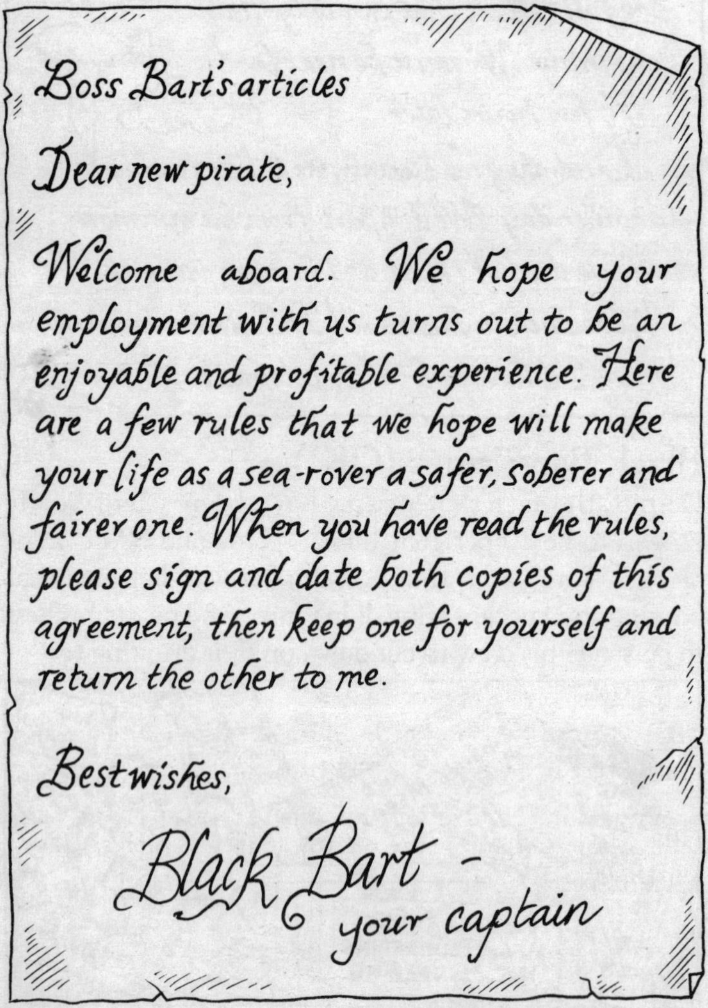

Boss Bart's articles

Dear new pirate,

Welcome aboard. We hope your employment with us turns out to be an enjoyable and profitable experience. Here are a few rules that we hope will make your life as a sea-rover a safer, soberer and fairer one. When you have read the rules, please sign and date both copies of this agreement, then keep one for yourself and return the other to me.

Best wishes,

Black Bart –
your captain

1. You'll get a fair share of all the drink and food we pinch. Plus a vote on whatever we're deciding to do next.

2. You'll also get an equal share of the loot. But, if you try to steal a bit extra, we'll maroon you! BTW: I get double shares ... cos I'm boss!

3. If you rob another pirate we'll slit your nose and ears (then try wearing your new sunglasses!) After that, we'll maroon you.

4. No gambling for money with dice or cards (but the odd game of snap or housey-housey is OK, as long as you're not too noisy).

5. Lights out at eight. If you want to drink after that, do it on deck in the dark.

6. Always keep your cutlass and pistols clean and ready for action.

7. No girlfriends allowed on board. Punishment for lady-smuggling: death.

8. If you run away during a battle, we'll kill you or maroon you.

9. Don't hit other pirates. If you want to settle a quarrel you can fight a duel on shore.

10. You can't retire until you've saved up £1,000.

11. If you get badly wounded, or lose a leg or arm, we'll give you 800 pieces of eight. If it's not as bad as that you won't get quite as much. (NB: Bangs on the head qualify for a lump sum.)

12. Musicians get Sunday off (or, if they're rubbish, the entire week).

Despite the fact that they'd signed the articles, Bart's crew were a stroppy lot and he sometimes found his control over his men pushed to breaking point.

Bart's Blog

Spring 1721: Haven't caught a prize for two weeks. And we're in a right state (yes, again!): overcrowded, stinking, ship's timbers rotting, hardly any food left. My pirates are getting stroppier by the minute. Arguing, moaning, sulking and fighting amongst themselves all the time. They've turned into a load of ungovernable brutes (and that's just the well-behaved ones).

GRR!

What with all this grumbling and muttering, I've made up my mind to act really tough. I've got this new walk. A sort of hardman swagger where I glare at them, giving them this sort of, 'Want some, do you? Well, make my day! If you think you're hard enough!' look. I've told them I'll go ashore and fight any of 'em with the swords and pistols if they're up for it.

Can't say I blame them for whinging though. It is awful on this manky ship. Just hope we see some action soon to take their minds off it all.

A few days later: This is all I need! Sent a load of pirates ashore to get fresh water today. As they were hauling the barrel up from the rowing boat, the rope broke and it fell right on top of one of them, knocking him senseless. Well, I went nuts! Gave the pirate whose fault it was a right telling-off. And what does he do? He only swears at me. Then spits on me. All over my lovely crimson tunic! So what did I do? I shot him dead. BANG! Just like that.

Well, you can't ignore that sort of thing. They'll all be at it if I do. But that's only the start of it. Not long afterwards, his mate Jones arrives back from water-collecting. When he sees I've killed his pal, he goes for me. So I runs him through with me sword! But even though he's got this dirty great hole in him, he whips out his dagger and fights back. I stumble and, next minute, he's got me bent over a cannon, belting the living daylights out of me! A load of pirates pulled him off, but it was a close thing. Then, after a load of shouting and arm-waving, my quartermaster, Simpson, gets control and decides Jones should be lashed for insulting me. So, as soon as he gets better from the sword wound, we're all gonna take turns whipping him - 2 lashes each - from all 180 of us! Good bloke that Simpson! Anyway, let's hope things look up and we soon take some prizes.

Fortunately for Bart, things did look up. But not so fortunately for his victims.

BLACK BART'S GREATEST HITS (Part two)

· A few days later: Martinique: Used captured Dutch boat to lure out 14 ships, us pretending to be there for trade. Then took their gold, tortured 'em and burned their ships. Ha!

· August 1721: Calabar, Nigeria: Tried to trade with locals. They refused when they found out we were pirates. So we had a scrap. Forty of us against 2,000 of them. We won.

· 11 January 1722: Ouidah: Captured 11 slave ships and demanded ransom of 8 pounds of gold dust for each one (altogether, about half a million pounds in today's money).

Enter the pirate hunter

Captain's Log RN

Spring 1721 - The newspapers are full of stories of the atrocities of that pirate blighter, Black Bart. He attacks who he likes and when he likes without fear of being caught. His raids are costing England and our allies dear. Now the authorities have decided that enough is enough. He is to be hunted down. And I've been given the job of catching him. So we're off to Africa. By the way, the name's Ogle, Captain Chaloner Ogle, British Royal Navy, at your service!

9 June 1721 Africa - Slight problem today. When we called at Cape Three Points for fresh water, some of my sailors were kidnapped by an African choppy called Johnny Conny. I had to pay him gold for their release. On entering his palace to hand over the ransom, I saw human jaw bones hanging from a tree in his courtyard! Then, to my horror, I noticed that his floor is made from human skulls. I later discovered they were those of Dutch sailors, slaughtered by Conny and his men! Seafaring is not an easy life.

WE WERE THINKING OF TERRACOTTA - BUT THESE ARE SO MUCH EASIER TO CLEAN

September 1721 - Principe Island: Still no sign of those blasted pirates. And now I have more troubles! While we have been here 50 of my sailors have died from the dreaded yellow fever.

DISGUSTING DISEASES — YELLOW FEVER

CAUSES: Being bitten by mosquitoes that have caught yellow fever from monkeys. Pirates got yellow fever because they hung out in the Tropics a lot.

SYMPTOMS: You get a rotten headache and backache and begin being sick all over the place. Then your temperature rockets and you sweat buckets. Your skin and the whites of your eyes turn yellow. This carries on for three days, after which, you either a) begin vomiting black blood and die or b) get better because your antibodies have helped you to fight off the fever, giving you lifelong resistance to it.

TREATMENT: Drink plenty of water, get lots of rest (and try to avoid wearing colours which clash with yellow).

Cure: None.

December 1721 - Everywhere we go, we come upon sailors whose ships have been looted and burned by Black Bart. But he is nowhere to be found!

15 January 1722 - Arrived at Ouidah to find the slave ship which was burned by Bart's men just two days ago. But now they've fled. We've missed the blighter again!

PS Just had a chat with an ex-pirate chappy who sailed with Bart. And he's mentioned Cape Lopez three times. Might be worth investigating?

Eat my shots, Bart!

In February 1722, Bart anchored his three ships at a lovely sandy beach at Cape Lopez on the African coast for a bit of careening, carousing and comfortable living. The pirates all felt good. The sun was shining, their treasure chests were full and there was fresh air, fruit and fish for free. They were relaxing, playing cards, drinking rum and dreaming of how they would soon be spending their huge personal fortunes. Then, as Bart sat on a clifftop overlooking the beach, enjoying his breakfast, he spotted a large ship heading into the bay. All at once, the ship turned away and began to make for the open ocean. It must be a merchant ship, thought Bart, and it was too good an opportunity to miss! He ordered Skyrme, the Captain of the *Ranger*, to give chase.

Captain's Log RN
February 1722-Bart didn't know it at the time, but the ship that had turned away was mine. My hunch about Cape Lopez had paid off. He was there! With his ships tilted for careening. What an opportunity! But now I was furious. My stupid steersman had run my ship, the Swallow, on to a sandbank! Which is why we'd turned away to make a second run into the bay. But what a bit of luck this proved to be! Next thing we knew, the Ranger was chasing us. Bring it on! I thought, ordering my chaps to make it look as though we really were running away, but slowly enough for the pirates to catch us.
And when they did, my cannon were ready for 'em!

As were my swivels, my muskets and my pistols. We blasted them! We raked them! We brought their main mast crashing to the decks. Shot ripped into flesh, making pirates howl with pain. Slivers of timber punctured their lungs while shards of white-hot metal tore off their limbs. One poor wretch had his leg blown off, but the brave fool simply carried on fighting with his stump gushing blood. However, victory was quickly ours. With ten pirates dead and another 20 badly wounded, they soon surrendered and were promptly arrested by me and my sailors. But I could not linger. I had to return to Cape Lopez with all speed before Black Bart realized things had gone so badly for his chums! And once there I intended to do the same to him as I had to Skyrme. Pulverize him with my cannon!

WICKED WEAPONS

Kerboom! Crash! Crunch!: The cannon

• Cannon: A cast-iron ball blasted from a cannon could hit a ship half a mile away, shattering its woodwork and bringing its mast, sails and rigging crashing to the decks. But it would take at least four pirates a minimum of three minutes to load, aim and fire the cannon then push it back into position after it had recoiled from the blast. One technique pirate gunners used was to 'bounce' their cannon balls off the surface of the sea, rather like you skim a stone across a pond.

Other things that were shot from cannon:
• Bar shot: Big iron bars made to puncture huge holes in a ship's woodwork.
• Chain shot: Small iron balls joined with chain or a small bar which spun as they flew through the air, shredding sails and rigging as they went.

YOU'RE SUPPOSED TO SHRED THE ENEMIES' RIGGING, JONES! NOT OURS

• Bundle Shot: Horrid little packs of short metal bars.
• Grape shot: Little cast-iron balls wrapped in canvas, which quickly turned victims into holey ghosts.
• Anything else the pirates could lay their hands on, including scrap iron, nails, spikes and even gold coins from their loot if they were really desperate. (After a battle, penny-pinching types would often cut the coins out of dead bodies.)

Swivel guns
These were a smaller type of cannon mounted on swivels so they could be swung this way and that, all depending on where the target happened to be. They fired smaller ammunition like grape shot and chain shot.

⚓ The Maritime Times ⚓

GOTCHA! OUR BRAVE BOYS BEAT BLACK BART IN BLOODY BATTLE

EAT MY SHOTS, BART!

Rejoice! Rejoice! That scourge of the seven seas, Black Bart Roberts, is dead! As you know, brave Captain Chaloner Ogle has been hunting Bart these last 12 months. Well, he finally found him at Cape Lopez, lured away his accomplice, Skyrme, defeated him, then returned to deal with Bart himself.

On the morning of 10 February, Bart was enjoying a salmagundi stew while his liquor-lout crew knocked back their own breakfasts of booze, biscuits, and more booze! Then, as the squiffy swashbucklers awaited the return of Skyrme, eager to get their share of the plunder they believed he would bring, a ship came into sight. As Bart raised his tea cup to his lips his eyes went wide with amazement. The ship entering the bay wasn't the *Ranger*. It was Captain Ogle's *Swallow*!

Leaping to his feet, Bart began yelling orders as his officers kicked and punched his pie-eyed pirates into action. By the time the *Swallow* had manoeuvred into the bay, Bart's ship, the *Fortune*, was floating out to meet her. But Bart didn't intend to fight. He knew his sozzled sailors were no match for the Royal Navy's finest. He planned to sail right past them and escape to the open sea.

As the two ships passed, the *Swallow*'s 20 cannon blasted a broadside into the *Fortune*, while small arms and swivel guns sent pellets and bullets whizzing amongst the pickled pirates! The *Fortune*'s mast was hit but she still headed for the open sea. But then, desperate to get himself out of range of the *Swallow*'s broadsides, the *Fortune*'s terrified helmsman steered her to starboard, right across her stern. Seconds later, the wind went out of the *Fortune*'s sails and the two ships once more came abreast of each other. Again, the *Swallow*'s cannon thundered, her swivels spat grape and chainshot, while brave sailors, high in her rigging, let fly with pistols and muskets.

As the smoke of battle cleared, the *Fortune*'s second mate spotted a figure crouched behind a cannon, clinging to its rope. It was Black Bart! Thinking his Captain had lost his nerve, he gave him a kick and yelled, 'Get up and fight like a man!' But, as he did, Bart's head flopped to one side and the mate saw the blood spurting from the huge hole that the grape shot had just made in his throat. The second mate immediately burst into tears and wrapped his arms around his dead leader, sobbing uncontrollably. Moments later he was joined by the quartermaster. The two heartbroken pirates hoisted up Bart's body and tipped it into the sea, just as he'd asked, should he ever be killed in battle.

For two more ear-splitting, stomach-churning hours, the battle raged, with just 20 pirates fanatically defending the *Fortune*, while the rest cowered in the hold. With dying pirates littering the decks, the cut-throats finally surrendered to Captain Ogle. And then, as the beaten buccaneers were clapped in irons, the heavens opened, thunder roared and a great flash of lightning struck the *Swallow*'s main mast, splitting it down the middle. Bart's revenge? Or a freak accident? Who knows? But reader, how spooky is that?

Of course the pirates will soon be sentenced to death and hanged. So if you want to read a really detailed and sickening account of all their squirming and groaning and see some really gruesome pictures … watch this space!

ALL IN A DAY'S WORK

When they bagged Bart and made him their captain,
those pirates probably breathed a huge sigh of relief. The
crews of pirate ships were organized in the same way as
those of merchant and navy vessels, with everyone on
board having special responsibilities. However, it was
really difficult to find determined and reliable people with
the specialist skills needed to keep a pirate ship afloat and
a crew happy, well-behaved and healthy. Which is why
Howell Davis's lads were so pleased when they found
someone as smart and courageous as Bartholomew.

If they hadn't captured him, they might well have had
to advertise for new staff at the pirate job centre...

SITUATIONS VACANT

WANTED: PIRATES

DUE TO QUITE A LOT
OF OUR STAFF HAVING
RECENTLY BEEN BLOWN
TO BITS, DROWNED, HUNG,
SHOT AND EATEN BY
SHARKS, WE HAVE THE
FOLLOWING VACANCIES:

Captain

Must be a COURAGEOUS and DARING LEADER. Would suit outright BULLY with no conscience whatsoever, who really enjoys seeing others suffer.

PERKS OF THE JOB: Double the amount of booty everyone else gets. Power of life or death over anyone taken prisoner. Free wooden leg (optional). NB: Expect your pirate crew to mutiny and replace you with someone else if you don't prove to be a courageous, cunning and canny leader who provides them with plenty of prizes and partying. Well, what do you expect? THEY'RE PIRATES!

Quartermaster

You'll be SECOND IN COMMAND and in charge of all the other pirates when your ship isn't in action. You must LEAD ATTACKS and be the first to leap on to the ship you're boarding. You'll also be in charge of food and water supplies, and do things like STEERING the ship, NAVIGATING and looking after the binnacle (the box housing the compass).

CAREER PROSPECTS: Excellent! If you capture a ship, you'll get to be its captain.

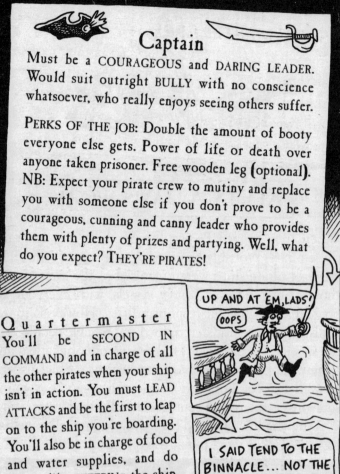

SHIP'S MASTER (also known as the Pilot)

You will be responsible for sailing the ship. You must know all about NAVIGATION and PILOTING. We really value your skills and, should you prove yourself to be competent, we will respectfully address you as the 'sea-artist'. NB: Must provide own maps and navigation instruments.

BOATSWAIN

You must inspect your ship's sails and rigging each morning and generally make sure your ship remains ship-shape.

You must also keep your ship stocked with supplies such as tar, pitch and tallow and spare sails. You will also be in charge of deck activities such as WEIGHING THE ANCHOR.

Master Gunner

You are to be responsible for the ship's GUNS and AMMUNITION. This includes sifting the powder to keep it dry and prevent it from separating, as well as ensuring the cannon balls are kept free of rust, and all weapons are in good repair. And of course, in battle your job will be a) to skilfully scare 'prizes' into surrendering by a well-placed shot across their bows, or b) to blast anyone who attacks us.

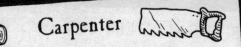

Carpenter

LET'S HOPE YOU LIKE BEING BUSY!
When you're not patching up all the cannon-ball holes, broken masts and burned woodwork we end up with after a battle, you'll be checking the hull for leaks, plugging the gaps between the planks, replacing rotting timbers, and repairing and replacing all the other things made of wood. In other words, almost everything on board! Oh, and did we mention WOODEN LEGS?

SURGEON
Your duties will include INSPECTING NEW RECRUITS to see if they're fit for the pirate life.

And of course, you'll be treating sick and wounded pirates, which means sawing off their arms and legs, sticking your hands where other hands dare not go, and regularly catching all manner of DISGUSTING DISEASES from your patients.

Cook

You'll be relieved to know us pirates aren't big on 5-STAR GOURMET CUISINE. Almost all your duties will consist of boiling huge quantities of meat in the massive cooking pot known as the STEEP TUB. You must also remember to lash down the steep tub in stormy weather.

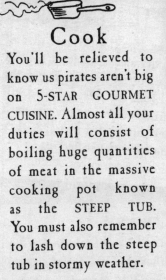

ORDINARY SEAMAN

You'll need to know the ropes ... and the sails, and the knots, and the names of all those ODD-LOOKING STICKY-OUT BITS that you find all over sailing ships. Why? Because you'll be all over the boat, setting sails, hauling ropes, turning the capstan, weighing the anchor, pumping out the bilges and scrambling up the rigging, as you make your way aloft to scan the horizon for victims (and collect the eggs from the crow's nest). You'll also need to be able to 'read' the weather, seas, skies and winds and be able to predict how any changes might affect your ship's progress.

Cooper

Your job's a real BARREL of laughs. You'll make sure that all the wooden containers for water, dry and salted food, pickled meat and fish are well sealed and watertight. If they're not, the food will go off, the water will leak and rats and mice will nibble our provisions. When a barrel becomes empty you must dismantle it into its staves and hoops for storage, then reassemble when it's needed again for water collecting.

POWDER MONKEY

If you're not expecting to get too far in life this job may well suit you. Or to put it another way, it's a bit of a dead end – in more ways than one! You'll be treated with less respect than the BILGE RATS, paid whenever it suits us (in other words, hardly ever) and be in constant danger. During the height of battle you'll be expected to scurry back and forth across the decks carrying GUNPOWDER from the stores to the cannons. This means you'll be a small human bomb who may EXPLODE into a thousand minced morsels at any moment. But that's only if you're lucky. You're more likely to be partly ripped apart by flying debris, shot through with a red-hot musket ball, or shredded by chain shot, after which you'll die slowly and agonizingly as your blood stains the ship's timbers crimson. But don't feel too bad about that, the sand your mates have so thoughtfully spread on the decks before the battle will soak up most of it.

ANNE BONNY AND HER FLAMING TEMPER 1697-?

Most pirates were men. Which only stands to reason, doesn't it? Whoever heard of a *woman* sailing around the world? Or, even more ridiculously, sailing around the world single-handedly? As if!

Despite this, very occasionally, some stupid, soppy girl *would* decide to become a pirate and go off 'on account', having decided she could beat the men at sea-roving.

COME ALONG, CHAPS! LET'S GO AND STEAL LOTS OF LOVELY SHOES AND DWESSES!

This chapter's all about the one-woman pirate whirlwind known as Anne Bonny, plus a few more feisty fighting females. Some of these astonishing women not only beat the men at their own game, but also made quite a few them look like complete wimps as well!

Wild-child

Anne's dad was an Irish lawyer and her mum was a serving-maid called Peg (who he apparently fancied more than his wife). When Anne was born in 1700, local people were so outraged about Mr Cormac and Peg's bit of hanky-panky that the two of them were forced to leave Ireland and take their new baby to South Carolina in America, to escape all the pointing fingers, raised eyebrows and wagging tongues.

Being a determined sort of chap, it wasn't long before Mr Cormac had set himself up as a lawyer again and he soon made enough money to buy an enormous house and country estate in Charleston, with lots of slaves to cook his new family's dinners, wash their dishes and shine their shoes.

It was Mr Cormac's hope that little Anne would grow up to become a 'lady' and marry someone rich and sophisticated. But Anne had different ideas. By the time she was a teenager, rather than going to society balls and mixing with young toffs, she was chilling with the local ragamuffins down at the docks and getting up to the sorts of things that would have landed her with an entire legful of electronic tags and enough ASBOs to wallpaper her bedroom (had those things existed in those days).

Her poor parents were beside themselves with worry. And things weren't helped by her hypersensitive mum's habit of swooning at the least little bit of excitement. Having a wild-child like Anne gave her lots of opportunities for dramatic flops-to-the-floor…

Anne's anti-social antics

• As a result of skipping school and hanging around with dockside delinquents, Anne soon became a really first-class swearer, regularly coming out with strings of oaths that would melt the ears off a brass elephant. Her dad said he didn't mind too much, but as for her mum…

• Young Anne made friends with a local native American Indian called Charley Fourfeathers and spent many happy hours racing around the woods with him, swimming rivers, climbing trees and wrestling squirrels. One day, in tribute to her pal, she shaved off most of her hair so that it looked exactly like his cool, native American topknot. Just as her mum was having a tea-party with the local ladies, Anne rushed into the room to show off her fab new 'hair-don't' and Mum responded in her usual faint-hearted fashion.

• Fortescue Kendal (a dashing young man, not a picturesque Cotswold village) was the son of a mega-rich South Carolina plantation owner. Fortescue was nuts about Anne, but she didn't fancy him one bit. Nevertheless, he boasted to his buddies that the two of them were having regular passion parties in local shacks and shrubberies. One day, he went to Anne's dad and mum and offered to marry her. This caused Anne's mum to faint. However, Anne's dad thought this was a great idea (the marriage, not the fainting). When he asked Anne what she thought, she smiled sweetly and said she'd like a few moments alone with Fortescue. Exchanging knowing grins, her mum and dad left the two 'lovebirds' alone.

A moment later they heard terrible screams, shouts and crashes. Mr Cormac rushed back into the room to find Anne beating the living daylights out of blabber-gob Fortescue, who now resembled a raw beefburger with triple tomato relish.

• One day at the dinner table Anne had a bit of a tiff with one of the family's servants, a big stroppy lass called Clara Hawkins. When clumsy Clara spilled gravy on her lap, Anne slapped her face and called her a very rude name, so Clara picked up a knife and waved it menacingly at Anne. However, Anne was too quick for her and, picking up her own knife, she stabbed Clara dead. (NB: It's not known if Anne then went on to finish the pudding course.)

Anne's Lost Diaries

20 March 1712 – Met a part-time pirate called James Bonny today. He's at least eight inches shorter than me, pastier than a shark's stomach and scrawnier than a shrimp. I've also heard folk say he's a fink and a snot-carrier*. But there is a certain something about him that rattles my jib.

15 April 1712 – I tryst with James in the upstairs back-room at the dockyard tavern every day. I just can't get enough of that certain something of his ... though I'll be jiggered if I know what it is. Today we decided to marry so that father will be forced to give me my inheritance. Then we can buy a sloop and go smuggling on our own account!

1 May 1712 – We are in North Carolina. And we are wed! By a minister we paid with rum.

* A government informer.

7 May 1712 - Yesterday my parents received word that we are man and wife. And, as usual ... mother fainted. But she didn't just faint, she died, too. I really am beside myself with sorrow.

10 May 1712 - James and I returned to Charleston today. Dear Mother is now in the cold, dark earth, buried yesterday. When we tried to talk to Father about my inheritance he refused to let us in the house, telling me I had 'murdered' Mother and was a 'child of sin'. As we stood on the doorstep pleading with him, a shot rang out and a musket ball passed through the front door, barely missing us! That pathetic, lily-livered husband of mine turned to run, but I tripped the cowardly dog, then cuffed him soundly about the ears. And then I saw red! Seizing stones and rocks, I began hurling them at my parents' house until every single

window was smashed. But that wasn't enough! Next, I seized James' tinder box, and, yelled, 'Father! I want my inheritance. I'll roast you out of there!' Then I set fire to the place. Soon flames were licking at the curtains that dangled from the broken windows and our slaves were running this way and that, trying to put out the fire. Now, more musket shots roared from the house and, as Father yelled, 'I've disinherited you! I'll have the military on you!' everyone dived for cover. At this moment, my loyal Indian chum, Charley Fourfeathers, appeared at my side and whispered, 'Better you go!' I saw he spoke sense and allowed him to lead us to this shack deep in the forest. Which is where I am now writing this diary. I wonder what tomorrow will bring?

Tomorrow brought Anne and James a new life. They upped sticks and sailed to New Providence in the Bahamas. Which just happens to be another of our...

147

New Providence suited Anne perfectly. The place was heaving with rogues of every sort, and she was soon carousing with cut-throats, boozing with buccaneers and partying with pirates. Pirates like Pierre Bousquet.

Pierre Bousquet – French pirate (the clue's in the name):

Claim to shame: Pierre was an ex-barber, actor, stage designer and dressmaker who stabbed someone during an argument.

He then became a ship's cook but once more his temper boiled over and he attempted to bone and fillet one of his fellow chefs.

Realizing they would hand him over to the authorities and have him hanged the moment they reached land he sprinkled rat poison on the dinners of the ship's captain and his mates (yes, folks, Pierre got his 'rataliation' in first).

When they dropped dead he took over the ship and not long afterwards met up with some pirates who were so impressed with the sheer pluck of this extra-stroppy cook that they took him back to New Providence where he met Anne, opened a restaurant (Le Rat Mort?) and eventually joined her pirate gang.

Anne's first big raid

Anne got wind of the fact that a merchant ship laden with fine fabrics and lovely clothes was due to pass through the Straits of Florida. She and Pierre planned to waylay it using a sloop that someone had carelessly left unattended in New Providence harbour.

Having togged themselves out in snazzy white blouses and tight black breeches, Anne and her gang proceeded to sling buckets of turtle blood over the sails of the sloop whilst spilling lots of it on themselves in the process. Next they stood one of Pierre's dressmaker's dummies on the bow (front-end in landlubber speak) of the sloop, dressed it in a magnificent, white evening gown and stuck a false head on top of it, after which they drenched the whole thing in more turtle blood.

With a drunken pirate at the wheel of the sloop they set off in search of the ship. By luck they quickly found it and had soon pulled alongside with Pierre playing a flute with one hand whilst waving his cutlass with the other and the other pirates tootling away on their musical instruments and generally looking rather intimidating. In the meantime, Anne was whirling an axe around her head, making it look as if she just walloped the poor blood-drenched 'woman prisoner' who stood in the sloop's bow.

At this point Pierre decided to fire the sloop's one cannon but unfortunately it blew up in his face. The huge cloud of smoke prevented the merchant ship's navigator from seeing where he was going so he crunched into the pirate ship.

After the smoke had cleared Anne and her pirates leapt aboard the merchant ship and began unloading the fab fabrics and cool clothes, while Pierre wrapped himself in a roll of silk and began excitedly twirling around the deck.

It wasn't long after this adventure that Anne met Calico Jack Rackham, the handsome, dashing, pirate dandy, with whom she would run away to sea and finally become a world-famous, full-time female pirate. But Anne wasn't the only girl who took up the pirate life. There were many others. So before we continue her amazing story, let's have a look at another fighting female sea-rover.

Mrs Cheng and her great big Chinese takeaway

Cheng I Sao means 'the wife of Cheng' or Mrs Cheng in other words. Mrs Cheng first met Mr Cheng in 1801 when he and his gang of Chinese pirates captured the ship she was travelling on. Mr Cheng had been looking for a wife for ages but, despite the fact that he was rich and powerful, he hadn't been able to find one. However, the moment he clapped eyes on the beautiful young woman who would soon become Mrs Cheng, he said something like 'Phwoar! You are one absolute cracker! I want to marry you, my crispy little Peking duckling!' And, in true feminist fashion, she responded by leaping on him and trying to gouge out his eyes. For reasons

known only to Mr Cheng, this impressed him no end, so he said, 'Now I want to marry you even more, my fragrant little lotus blossom! I'll give all the tea in China if you'll say "yes"!' But still the lovely young woman continued to tear at Mr Cheng's throat with her talon-like nails, so he said something like, 'Oh my little fire-breathing dragon, I love you to pieces. I'll give you anything you ask!' So she instantly calmed down and said, 'Oh all right then, if you give me a 50 per cent slice of your massive pirate empire, I'll be your Mrs!'

'Done!' said Mr Cheng, and soon he and Mrs Cheng were rampaging around the coasts and rivers of South China with their 400 junks and 50,000-strong pirate army, plundering, persecuting and pulverizing. However, pirating being a perilous pastime, Mr Cheng was killed in action in 1807, leaving Mrs Cheng to take over the family business and marry her stepson, Chang Pao, who also became her partner in crime.

So off they went, with their Red Flag Fleet, as it was now known, ransacking villages, capturing merchant ships and 'taxing' fishing boats and fellow pirates alike. Cheng and Chang soon got themselves a reputation for carrying out all manner of cruel and violent acts. For instance, when they attacked the village of Sanshan in 1809, they cut off the heads of all 80 of the local men and hung them from a banyan tree, because they thought they'd conspired with their enemies.

Mrs Cheng wasn't much nicer to her pirates. If they went off duty without permission, she chopped off their ears, and if they tried to pinch the plunder, she cut off their ears and their heads. Pirates caught canoodling on board were also beheaded (but may well have been allowed to keep their ears).

I SAID LEAVE THE EARS. JUST CUT OFF THE HEAD! CAN'T YOU DO ANYTHING RIGHT?

The Chinese government and its navy were powerless to stop Mrs Cheng and her ever-growing army of cut-throats, so they went to the British and Portuguese governments for help, as they too were having their ships attacked and their trade with China disrupted. With a fleet of British and Portuguese warships standing by, the Chinese Emperor invited Mrs Cheng to a pow-wow, where she was greeted like a sea-roving superstar with music and cannon salutes. Then, as soon as they'd finished fussing and grovelling, the Emperor's officials said to Mrs Cheng, 'Look Mrs Cheng, old love, here's the deal! You stop pirating and hand over all your weapons and ships and we'll let you and your 50,000 pirates off all the murdering, pillaging, torturing and burning you've all been doing for the last nine years. In addition to which, we'll let you keep all the stuff you've nicked *and* we'll give you a palace to live in and Chang a high-up job in the Chinese army! How does that grab you? Mrs Cheng was no fool. She knew it was an offer she couldn't refuse, so she immediately said...

...and lived the rest of her life in luxury.

Right, it's time we got back to Anne and James and Jack. And, after all that beheading and whatnot, it's also time to calm things down a bit. Why not with a short romantic interlude? So, here's a charming...

Love story

Once upon a time there were some young people called Anne, Jack, Mary, Mark and James.

Jack was nuts about Anne. And she thought he was wonderful, too. But Anne was married to James. So Jack went to see James.

'I love your wife. Divorce her so that I can marry her!' he said.

'Get lost, fish-face!' replied James. 'She's mine, and that's that!'

Jack thought for a moment, then said, 'Look, I tell you what. I'll buy her off you. How much do you want?'

'What!' gasped James, truly shocked by Jack's outrageous offer. 'How dare you? I'm going to tell the governor on you!'

Which he did. And, not long afterwards, the governor told Jack and Anne that if they didn't put a stop to their affair, he'd have them both whipped

'Oh, stuff this for a game of pirates!' said Jack and Anne. 'It's a dead loss!'

And with that they stole a ship and went off pirating, spending the next a couple of years having lots of fun and making a general nuisance of themselves around the Caribbean.

One day they captured a Dutch merchant ship and several of its crew joined their band of pirates. One of them, a young chap called Mark, soon caught Anne's eye.

'Hmm, what a hunk!' she thought. 'I wouldn't mind rattling *his* jib!'

So, one day, when the other pirates were boozing and snoozing, Anne sidled up to Mark and said something like, 'Hi dreamboat, how's about you and me making some pirate rock and roll? And by the way, I'm not a chap. I'm a girl, pretending to be a chap. I only dress like this for work!'

To which Mark replied, 'Well, I don't wish to be spoilsport or anything ... but I'm not a chap either! I'm also a girl pretending to be a chap! My name's Mary Read. Let's be friends!'

BRILLIANT! AT LAST, SOMEONE TO TALK TO ABOUT SHOES!

Scary Mary

Mary Read's mum had been married to a sea captain who went off to work one day and never came back, due to the fact that he'd been killed in a sea battle, drowned, swallowed by a whale, or something like that. Not long after this, the newly widowed Mrs Read had a brief romantic fling with another chap and gave birth to Mary. However the chap ran off and Mrs Read ran out of money. So, dressing little Mary as a boy in order to claim 'his' inheritance, she went to her mother-in-law in London and said to Granny Read...

THIS IS YOUR LITTLE GRANDSON MARK. WE'RE STARVING AREN'T WE, MARY? SORRY I MEAN MARK! PLEASE GIVE US SOME MONEY.

So Gran agreed to give them a crown every week (a crown coin, not a shiny pointy hat) to keep little 'Mark' in trousers, boxer shorts, hobnail boots (and trainer bras). But of course, in order to fool Gran, Mary had to carry on dressing up as a little boy (well, it was either that or hide Gran's spectacles).

When Mary was 13, her mum got her a job with a posh French lady. Not as a maid or serving wench, but as a little footman, complete with flunky's outfit and cheesy stick-on grin. But, by this time, Mary had grown up to be a strong, lively and adventurous lass/lad and soon became bored with bowing and scraping. She decided she'd be something more funky than a flunky, and ran away to join the Navy. Then, after having been a sailor for a bit, she ran away and joined the Army (and would have no doubt run away and joined the RAF, too … but it hadn't been invented).

The Army sent her to fight abroad and she soon got noticed by her commanding officers as she courageously distinguished herself on the battlefield.

She also found herself sharing her tent with a handsome young soldier and quickly fell in love with him. Soon, no longer able to contain herself, Mary said…

Not long afterwards, Mary and her sweetheart got married, opened a little pub and lived quite happily for a few years. But then Mary's husband died and the pub went out of business. Once more, Mary was penniless. It was time for her to dress up as a man again. So, having pulled on her trousers, boots and Y fronts, 'Mark' got a job on a Dutch merchant ship which was captured by some pirates. And the rest is history – or *her* story – or *our* story!

After they'd found out that they were both ladies pretending to be chaps, Anne and Mary became firm friends. They also turned out to be the most courageous pirates on Jack's boat, being the first to board prize ships and always fighting fearlessly, even when the odds were against them and their male mates were wetting themselves with terror. And when they'd reduced their opponents to snivelling wrecks, the two bosom buddies would whip off their shirts, just to make sure the snivelling seafarers knew that they'd been beaten by a couple of big girls (without) blouses.

Then, in a bold and daring move that would prove to be their undoing, Jack and Anne and Mary snuck into New Providence harbour and pinched a ship called the *William*. When he heard of this, Woodes Rogers – yes that bloke who had privateered all those years ago with brainy buccaneer, William Dampier and who was now the governor of New Providence and dedicated to ridding it of pirates – said to the Royal Navy…

Go get 'em!

Captain John Barnet decided the only way to beat the pirates was to attack them in a small sloop rather than a big warship, so that he could follow them into the bays and coves where they normally skedaddled when things warmed up. With his sailors dressed in the outfits of ordinary seamen, his Navy flags hidden away and his cannon concealed in the bow of his sloop, he went pirate-hunting.

Meanwhile, Jack and his pirates, up to their usual tricks, had caught a turtle-fishing boat and its cargo of four turtles and a large barrel of rum. They were now anchored in a small inlet, partying like there was no tomorrow (which, for most of them, would turn out to be true).

But Anne and Mary spotted Captain Barnet's sloop entering the bay and, realizing it meant trouble, immediately prepared to meet him and his men in mortal combat, loading their pistols, unsheathing their cutlasses (and frantically checking their lipstick). But, to their fury, their sozzled male shipmates simply scurried below decks and took refuge in the hold.

Mary instantly became an irate pirate and began firing her gun into the hold where the lily-livered lot now cowered in terror.

But then Captain Barnet and his men began swarming aboard the *William*, so Anne and Mary had no choice but to turn their attentions to them. And, as you might expect, they fought just like ... *a pair of BIG GIRLS!* ... furiously stabbing, shooting and slashing at their foes for all they were worth. But they were soon outgunned and outnumbered. Within minutes, the battle was over.

Along with the rest of the pirates, Anne and Mary were clapped in irons then taken back to Port Royal and locked in the damp, dismal dungeons deep beneath the fortress. Jack and the other chaps were the first to be brought before the courts. On the day of their trial, one witness after

another stepped forward to testify about the dastardly deeds that Jack and his poxy pirates had visited upon them.

There was no doubt about it. The men who stood before them were pirates! All 11 of them were found guilty and sentenced to be hanged by their necks until they were dead. And they were! As soon as they were well and truly throttled, Jack's body was cut down and put in a cage, which was taken to Dead Man's Cay and hung from a post as a warning to everyone entering Port Royal.

And then it was Anne and Mary's turn to face the courts. Again, they were accused of all sorts of sinful stuff, including stealing, stabbing, shooting and swearing in a way that was most shocking.

They too, were found guilty and sentenced to be hanged. But then, they delivered their bombshell…

'We're pregnant!' cried Mary.

So that was that! The judge had no choice but to let them off. After all, it wouldn't have been fair on the two tiny pirates who were no doubt already jiggling and wriggling inside them, desperate to be off plundering. So they were pardoned. Unfortunately, Mary died just a few days later from a fever she'd caught in the dungeons. But as for Anne, no one knows what became of her. Some people say that her rich dad took her back with him to live on his estate so that his new grandchild would have a safe and secure future. Others believe that she simply retired to live the difficult and selfless life of a single mum. But no one knows for sure.

However, despite disappearing into anonymity, Anne was to become an inspiration to other women pirates. Women pirates like…

Sadie the Goat
Sadie the Goat was a river pirate who lived in the roughest, grottiest part of New York in the nineteenth century. She began her life of crime as a land-lubbing mugger with a unique technique. Spotting a likely looking victim, she would crouch down, then charge at them, head-butting them in the stomach with such ferocity that her gang could simply pounce on them and relieve them of their cash, chequebooks, jewellery (and steam-powered iPods). Which, of course, was why she was called Sadie the Goat (as opposed to Sadie the Stick Insect, or Sadie the Giant Panda).

When she wasn't busy nutting passers-by, Sadie liked to spend her time in a pub called the Hole-In-The-Wall. This was an extremely rowdy and violent place, which was supervised by an enormous truncheon-toting, gunslinging lady bouncer called Gallus Mag. When someone misbehaved, Mag was in like a shot! After giving them a hefty clout with her cosh, she would firmly grasp their ear in her teeth, drag them to the door and throw them out. Or, if she was feeling really snappy, she wouldn't bother with the dragging bit, but would simply bite off the troublemaker's ear, then drop it in a jar, along with all the other ears she'd bitten off during her long and violent car*ear*.

One day, during a kerfuffle at the Hole-In-The-Wall, Mag bit off Sadie's ear. Sadie was so upset by this awful exp-*ear*-ience that she upped sticks and moved to another part of New York, where she took over a mob of river pirates called the Charlton Street Gang. With her new gang, Sadie began sneaking aboard ships moored in New York's docks and pinching their cargoes (having found head-butting them far too painful). After wrapping their oars in rags, Sadie and her fellow pirates, Flabby Brown, Big Mike and Big Brew, would row their little boat for miles, hidden under the quayside piers of the North River, as they looked for ships to rob.

Then, as soon as they spotted an unguarded 'prize', they would shin up its anchor chain, swipe everything they could, and sell their loot in the pubs and pawn shops of New York.

However, Sadie soon became discontented with these small-time raids. Being an avid reader of pirate books and a keen student of pirate history, she longed to be a proper pirate with pirate ship of her own, so that she could do some real swashbuckling, just like her heroes, Anne Bonny,

Mary Read and Blackbeard. To this effect, she and her gang swapped their pathetic little rowing boat for a top-of-the-range sloop, hoisted their own pirate flag and sailed off up the Hudson River in search of adventure and free money.

They were soon stopping off at lonely farmhouses and riverside mansions, robbing the occupants and doing lots of dastardly pirate stuff like plundering, kidnapping and making their victims walk the plank.

But Sadie's proper pirating career was short-lived. Being a river pirate, you can't just hightail it for the open seas or swap oceans when the going gets rough. Farmers and landowners quickly got wise to her hit-and-run tactics. Whenever her gang turned up, they were soon met by hordes of angry country people, all armed to the teeth with guns and pitchforks. Realizing that her pirating days were over, Sadie went back to head-butting and street robbery.

But one good thing did come out of all this. Sadie was reunited with her ear! The Hole-In-The-Wall had closed and Gallus Mag had lost her job. So, suddenly finding herself unemployed, broke (not to mention, up to her debt in ears), Mag gave Sadie her missing organ back. From that day on, Sadie lugged her ear about in a locket she wore around her neck (after it kept falling off when she tried to stick it back on with blu-tak).

BLACKBEARD AND HIS BLAZING BRISTLES 1680–1718

Blackbeard is probably the most famous pirate of them all. Not because he captured more ships than anyone else. Or stole more treasure than anyone else. Nor because he was more cruel or violent than any of his fellow swashbucklers. No, the reason people know about Blackbeard is because of the way he *looked*! Yes, his hideous image! Just one glimpse of this enormous, terrifying monster of a man would be enough to make battle-hardened sea-rovers throw down their cutlasses and beg for mercy. Which was great for Blackbeard, because it meant that, more often than not, he could capture a ship by simply turning up and looking really hard. And that would mean he and his pirates wouldn't have to get involved in all that inconvenient and painful fighting and stuff! Like most pirates, they didn't go out of their way to get involved in punch-ups. What they wanted was the easy life, i.e. minimum effort, lots of fun, and tons and tons of free money. What's more, Blackbeard knew he looked scary, and actually took lots of trouble to give himself the ultimate ferocious pirate makeover.

How to attain this season's ultimate 'Blackbeard' look

Become extremely ugly.

· Wear black clothes and black-knee boots all topped off with an enormous black hat (preferably soaked in some sort of fire retardant).

· Grow a massive black beard the size of Sherwood Forest. Let it spread all over your face. But don't forget to leave spaces for your mouth, nose and eyes.
· Make sure it's always good and filthy and twist it into hundreds of dreadlocks. Tie coloured ribbons to the locks.

· Grow your hair long, then twist that into dreadlocks too: preferably filthy.

· Grow incredibly tall. Get really big all over – huge shoulders, muscles on your muscles...

· Accessorize your outfit with:
a) a shoulder sling supporting three holsters containing pistols; b) a broad belt with daggers, cutlasses, more pistols and any other weapons you fancy tucked into it; c) some brightly coloured silk sashes.

Set your head on fire

Well not quite. The trick is to give the 'appearance' that your head is on fire. This is easily done by soaking lengths of rope in lime water and saltpetre then weaving them into your beard and hairdo. All you have to do then is set fire to them just before you show up at a confrontation. They'll smoulder at about 30 centimetres per hour so there should be no danger of you embarrassingly 'going out' during an attack. Important safety note: After a day's terrorizing, remember to extinguish yourself before going to bed.

Blackbeard: the murky years

Most people seem to think that Blackbeard was born around 1680 in the English port of Bristol. Or possibly London. Or the American city of Philadelphia. Or behind a wheely bin in Milton Keynes. In other words, no one's entirely sure where he came from. And, like so many of our other Horribly Famous pirates, absolutely nothing is known about his early life. However, we can be certain of one thing: he wasn't called Blackbeard to begin with, small babies with huge beards being quite rare (even in places like Bristol).

What he was called was Edward Drummond. Or Edward Teach. Or Edward Thatch. Or something like that. Again, no one's entirely sure. The thing is, if you're going to be a pirate, it's a good idea to have at least one false name. That way, when you get too old to swash your buckle, you can retire to a cottage in the country without fear of being tracked down.

172

What is known for certain about Blackbeard is that by the time he was 36 he had his own boat and pirate crew. So it can be more or less assumed that he had spent most of his life at sea, learning the ropes. Becoming an expert sailor isn't the sort of thing you pick up after an afternoon on your inflatable.

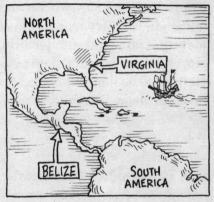

Blackbeard's reign of terror lasted a brief 18 months but, during this time, he and his 400-strong pirate gang terrorized all the seas between Belize and Virginia, capturing 40 ships and tons of plunder.

Soon the mere mention of his name was enough to strike panic into the hearts of seafarers and landlubbers alike. His beard alone was once described as 'a great meteor which terrified all America'.

And then there was his famous flag, one glimpse of which would reduce grown men to tears.

Stark waving bad: pirate flags – scary symbols and eye-catching icons

Before the invention of telephones and computers, communications between ships at sea was really difficult. So when you saw a boat in the distance it was hard to tell who it belonged to, and whether it was friendly or unfriendly. This is why a system of flags was developed for identification and for passing messages. The main purpose of most pirates' flags was to terrify their intended victims to the point where they'd surrender the moment they saw them. They'd do this by sending 'We are evil! And we know where you live!' sorts of messages.

Lots of really successful pirates (like Blackbeard) got very creative with their flags, designing personal logos that included bleeding hearts, blazing balls, spears, hourglasses, cutlasses and skeletons, usually on a black or red background. All these 'symbols' contained 'messages' for their enemies and lots of thought went into designing flags that would have the maximum impact on the crews of potential 'prizes'.

Most people think of the familiar 'skull and crossed bones' flags as a typical pirate banner. But the image was originally dreamed up to symbolize death in general and was used on the gravestones of all sorts of people, most of whom had never swashed a buckle. Which of course, could cause all sorts of confusion.

Here's a selection of flags and what they mean. (Two of them are completely made up though.)

False-colour flags: Flags belonging to other countries, flown to fool victims into believing there was nothing to worry about and therefore no need to run away.

Hourglass flag: Time is running out, lads. Surrender or we attack!

Black and white flag: OK! You've have your chance to surrender. Now we're gonna get you! This is the one the pirates raised if you didn't lower your flag to indicate that you intended to surrender.

Chequered flag: Congratulations! You've just come first in the Monaco Motor Racing Grand Prix. Though how you managed to do it in an eighteenth-century sailing ship is anyone's guess.

Red and white flag: We are a particularly nasty and cruel bunch of sea yobs. And when we catch you we'll kill the lot of you. So say your prayers!

Pink satin flag with green polka dots and purple taffeta frill: Actually, we're designer pirates and when we catch you we're going to give your ship such a fab makeover that even your own captain won't recognize it!

Bleeding-heart flag: You are going to die a particularly slow and painful death.

Horned-skeleton flag: We'll kill you. But before we do, we'll probably torture you!

176

So now you won't have any trouble working out what these Horribly Famous pirates' flags mean, will you?

BLACKBEARD'S FLAG

BLACK BART'S FLAG

BLACK BART HAD OTHER FLAGS INCLUDING THIS

A BARBADIAN'S HEAD (WE HATE BARBADIANS)

YES, BART WASN'T TOO KEEN ON PEOPLE FROM THE WEST INDIAN ISLANDS OF MARTINIQUE AND BARBADOS

ABH AMH

CALICO JACK RACKHAM

THOMAS TEW

A MARTINIQUAN'S HEAD (WE HATE MARTINIQUANS)

STEDE BONNET

CHRISTOPHER CONDENT

HENRY AVERY

CHRISTOPHER MOODY

Blackbeard's dreadful deeds

As Blackbeard pillaged here and murdered there, stories of his horrible personal habits and dreadful deeds were soon being told up and down America's Atlantic coast. Stories like these…

• Blackbeard was once sitting drinking with his navigator, Israel Hands, when, without warning, he pulled out his pistols and shot Israel in the knee. When asked why he'd done it, he said something like…

• Blackbeard and his crew were serial boozers. His favourite drink was rum … with a dash of gunpowder!

• One day, when he was feeling particularly playful and chatting with his pirates about him and them all eventually going to Hell because they were so wicked, Blackbeard suddenly roared…

'We're up for it boss!' yelled a couple of his more adventurous pirates and the three of them went down into the ship's hold and had themselves locked in with several pots of burning sulphurous brimstone.

After enduring the suffocating fumes for ages, the two pirates yelled, 'Help, let us out of here!' while Blackbeard simply sat there grinning.

• Whenever Blackbeard met a young lady he fancied, he'd make her his wife (or 'her onshore', as he no doubt called her). However, because he fancied such a huge amount of young ladies, he ended up with at least 14 different wives.
• Using his fleet of six pirate ships and 400 fearsome fighters to blockade the port of Charleston in South Carolina, Blackbeard took a prominent citizen and his four-year-old son hostage. He then threatened to decapitate them and send their heads to the Governor if he didn't give him a big chest of medicine.
• Once he got the medicine plus heaps of plunder, Blackbeard sailed out of Charleston, then pulled a fast one on his own pirates. Deliberately running his ship on to a sandbar, he marooned some of them, then fled the others, taking all the plunder and medicine with him.

But Blackbeard's successes weren't just down to his scary reputation – he was also a skilled seafarer and a super-smart strategist. And he certainly knew the ins and outs of...

How to take a prize: the ultimate guide to high-seas hijacking – top tips 'n' tactics

1 The most important thing to remember is that even though you're likely to have a bit of a battle with your victims, you don't want to seriously damage or sink the ship you're attacking. There wouldn't be any point, would there?

2 Spot your prey before they spot you. So, always keep lookouts posted. From the top of your 30-metre mast, a good lookout can clock a ship from 30 kilometres away.

3 'Stalk' your intended victims for days so that you can find out things like how many crew they have, what cargo they might be carrying, what guns they have and whether they're accompanied by warships.

4 Attack when they're least expecting it. Speed and surprise are your best allies. Your ship must be fast with nothing to slow it, such as barnacles or limpets stuck to its hull. So remember, always keep your bottom really clean (*and* your ship's bottom, for that matter).

5 Hide in a bay then ambush victims as they tootle past.
6 Sneakily row across to your target and jam the rudder (i.e. make its steering gear inoperative).
7 Put your victims off their guard by flying a false flag and pretending that you're from the same country as them. Then, as soon as you're good and close, whip up your pirate flag and blast a single shot across their bow. The other lot should be so gobsmacked that they instantly 'strike their colours' (lower their flag) and surrender without a peep.
8 Pretend you've come to help your victim in the battle against those awful pirates you've heard are coming to get them. Then, when they're feeling all relaxed and trusting, kill them and steal their possessions.

Black Bart's old boss, Howell Davis, used this technique. But someone turned the tables on him by pretending they were *his* friend, then killing *him* (ha!).

Go get him!

Eventually, as with all the bad boys and girls of the seven seas, Blackbeard's audacious activities got to be too much for the authorities. The Governor of Virginia put a pirate-hunter on his trail. Lieutenant Maynard of the British Royal Navy was sent to track him down and bring him to justice. It wasn't too hard to find him. Lieutenant Maynard located him at Ocracoke Creek, one of his favourite hangouts. Blackbeard was expecting him. But instead of hightailing it for the high seas, he stayed to fight in an action that would become known as one of the most bloody and dramatic battles in pirate history.

Blackbeard's Log:
Thursday 22 November 1718

It's dawn at Ocracoke Creek. Bit of a hangover this morning. Me and the lads got completely plastered last night. Come to think of it, we get completely plastered every night!

The two Royal Navy sloops are advancing on us now. But they have no cannon, only small arms and swords. What fools! And we're ready for them - our eight cannon are loaded. Soaked blankets have been hung around the powder magazine to protect it from sparks and to smother fires. And my boys are desperate for a scrap. We'll cut our anchor and lure them on to the sandbanks. Unlike them, I know these channels like the back of my hand. I'll lead these Royal Navy dogs a merry dance!

Ten minutes later: Ha! Got them! They're on the sandbanks and are well and truly stuck. They're sitting ducks. It's time to blast them to pieces.

sssss

But Lieutenant Maynard had other ideas. He was prepared for a savage conflict that would involve furious hand-to-hand fighting. And the use of all sorts of horrible weapons, including ones that were at the cutting edge of seagoing warfare!

WICKED WEAPONS

Up close and painful

• Cutlass: Sort of sword but shorter with broad, strong, curved blade that was probably developed from the buccaneers' hunting knife. It was ideal for shipboard hand-to-hand 'tight-spot' scraps because longer, normal 'swords' got tangled in rigging (and didn't look half as piratey). Pirates had no need to stop to reload either, they just chopped, lopped and topped. The cutlass was also handy for cutting down doors, slicing through ropes and dividing pieces of eight (not to mention trimming beards, picking teeth and cleaning fingernails).

• Dagger: Small knife with a 'hilt' to stop pirates slicing off their own fingers and to protect their hands from their opponent's cutlass blade. Used for thrusting and jabbing. It was small enough to hide inside clothing for a surprise attack. Good for below-deck scraps too. Pirates also used their daggers to pick up chunks of meat from their dinner plates.

• Crows' feet (aka caltrops): Pirates threw them on to the decks of the ships they were boarding. Sailors worked with bare feet to stop them slipping on wet decks, so caltrops usually left them hopping mad.

• Boarding hook with rope: Pirates used these to hook the ships they were about to board, pull them close and tie them to their own ship.

• Boarding axe: Essential, all-purpose weapon with a metre-long handle, sharp blade and blunt bit for hammering. Pirates used their versatile boarding axes to…

a) cut the ropes of boarding hooks.

b) chop down masts and cut rigging ropes which were often as thick as a man's arm.

c) smash through hatches, doors and locks to get at treasure.

d) pull themselves up the sides of big ships.

e) chop hot cannon balls out of woodwork to prevent a fire.

f) cut through fallen rigging and drag it out of the way.

g) bash people up.

• Tomahawk: Small axe which pirates liked to throw at people.

• Marlinespike: Knife-like tool made from steel, wood, or bone for unravelling and cutting rigging and ropes. Not really intended as a weapon, but many a stroppy pirate or mutinous sailor would often happen to have one in his hand when he fell out with an over-bossy captain and, as all the other weapons were always kept locked away until just before a battle, he'd think… 'Oh well, why not?'

• Hand grenade (named after *grenadoes* – the Spanish word for the pomegranate fruit): Small glass bottles or wooden, iron or clay pots containing gunpowder, broken glass and iron scraps. Pirates lit the fuse with a burning taper then threw it at their victims.

• Stinkpot: Small clay pot filled with burning sulphur, tar, rotten fish and any other horrid stuff pirates could lay hands on. They threw them on to the decks of the ship they were about to board so that the smelly gas left their victims coughing and spluttering so much that they forgot to fight.

Showdown at Ocracoke Creek

This is Abe Seaman reporting live for CNN (Colonial Nautical News) from Ocracoke Inlet. And I'm afraid I have to bring you bad news. An enormous broadside from Blackbeard's cannons has just hit Lieutenant Maynard's sloop. Its deck is littered with dead and dying sailors! And he's still desperately trying to free his ship from the sandbar. Smashing in barrels of water! Dumping everything he can! And yes, at last … they're moving.

A breeze has sprung up, pushing the *Jane* towards Blackbeard's *Adventure*. The two ships are closing. It will only be a matter of seconds before they meet. Just yards to go! And Blackbeard's back on the attack! His men are hurling grenades. Jagged, red-hot metal is flying in all directions. Surely this will be the end of brave Lieutenant Maynard and his men.

There's smoke everywhere. The ships are touching now. I can hear the clank of grappling irons. And yes! The enormous figure of Blackbeard has just made a massive leap and boarded Maynard's sloop.

'They were all knocked on the head but three or four!' I hear him cry to his cut-throats. 'Blast you! Board her and cut them to pieces!'

There must be at least ten pirates on board now! With more following. I fear the battle is lost.

But what's this? Incredible! Amazing! I don't believe it. And from the look of Blackbeard and his mob, I don't think they do! Royal Navy sailors are rushing up from the hold of the *Jane*, firing as they do. And now they're in amongst the pirates, shooting and hacking and stabbing at them whilst giving bloodcurdling battle yells. All bravely led by gallant Lieutenant Maynard!

Blackbeard and his men are now giving as good as they get. WHAT A SCRAP! Every now and again, a wounded pirate or sailor lets out a great scream, clutches a horrible wound and topples into the water. The sea is turning red with their blood. BANG! BANG! BANG! Pistols flash and men stagger backwards, grasping torn and bloodied flesh, whilst roaring in agony. And in the middle of this great struggling mass, I can see the gigantic figure of Blackbeard, slashing wildly with his cutlass and bellowing like a huge black bull. Every now and again he draws a pistol, fires, hurls away the spent weapon, then goes back to chopping and hacking at his foes.

HE'S BIGGER THAN HE LOOKS IN THE 'WANTED' POSTERS, ISN'T HE?

But what's this? Blackbeard and Captain Maynard are face to face, pistols drawn! Two shots ring out! Thank goodness… Lieutenant Maynard is OK!

But Blackbeard is shot! The monster of the seas is shot. Hurrah! Hurrah!

But wait! He's still on his feet. Despite being ripped open by a bullet he's fighting more fiercely than ever, chopping ferociously at Maynard with his cutlass as this brave Royal Navy officer desperately defends himself with his sword.

Oh calamity! Disaster! Blackbeard has broken off the blade of Lieutenant Maynard's sword. The officer is now at his mercy. Blackbeard is raising his cutlass for the killer blow. Lieutenant Maynard is trying to draw his pistol. But too late. Suddenly, blood is spurting from a huge crimson gash in his neck. No, NOT the Lieutenant's neck. I mean BLACKBEARD'S neck!

A Royal Navy sailor has slashed open Blackbeard's throat with his broadsword. Roaring with pain and rage, the pirate captain is lashing this way and that, as more and more sailors surround him. More pistol shots ring out and blood spurts from Blackbeard as great holes open up in his chest and legs. But still he fights on. Sailors are thrusting their swords into him over and over again. Is this man unkillable? He snarls, he curses and, as more wounds appear on his body, he strikes wildly at them, like a great bear being torn to pieces by dogs. Surely he can't last much longer. He's staggering now. He pulls out his one remaining pistol. Raises it to fire. But instead, he lets out a huge groan and slumps to the deck. As Lieutenant Maynard and his men look on, he twitches, shudders from head to toe and is still. The scourge of the seas is dead. Blackbeard is done for!

So that was that. Blackbeard finally got what was coming to him. And seeing their leader slain, his men soon gave up the fight, throwing down their guns and cutlasses and hurling themselves into the crimson sea. The battle was over. Blackbeard lay dead, with no less than 20 deep sword wounds in his body, five gaping bullet wounds and numerous other cuts and bruises. It had taken that much to kill him.

Just to be entirely sure that Blackbeard wouldn't suddenly jump up and start scrapping again, Lieutenant Maynard had his head cut off, then dangled it from the bow sprit of his ship.

DO YOU WANT ME TO KEEP AN EYE OUT FOR SANDBARS?

More excitable, over-imaginative (and profoundly stupid) witnesses said that Blackbeard's headless body jumped into the sea and swam around the boat several times. However, most sensible people believe this to be untrue.

BRITANNIA RULES ... AND THE PIRATES PERISH!

Around the time that Blackbeard, Black Bart and Calico Jack were meeting their gruesome ends, the period in history that some people (who've obviously never been pirates' victims) romantically refer to as 'The Golden Age of Piracy', was drawing to a close. The Royal Navy was on the case and, spurred on by brave buccaneer-bashers like Woodes Rogers, Captain Ogle and Lieutenant Maynard, they pulled out all the stops in order to rid the Caribbean and other areas of the pirate menace.

And it wasn't just Blackbeard, Black Bart and Calico Jack Rackham who got what was coming to them. Between 1716 and 1726, more than 400 pirates were captured, brought before the courts, found guilty and strung up in front of huge crowds of cheering onlookers. Then their bodies were dipped in tar and displayed in and around ports while their miserable confessions were printed and sold on the streets. All this publicity had the desired effect. Sailors began to think twice about giving up their day jobs and taking up a life of rum, rampaging and roistering. And, as a result, merchant ship captains everywhere were finally able to breathe a huge sigh of relief! At last, the Royal Navy ruled the waves, not the pirates. It was finally safe to go back in the water.